T0196046

MY
Delicious Life
WITH
Paula Deen

MICHAEL GROOVER

with Sherry Suib Cohen

SIMON & SCHUSTER
New York • London • Toronto • Sydney

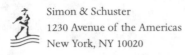
Simon & Schuster
1230 Avenue of the Americas
New York, NY 10020

First Simon & Schuster hardcover edition November 2009

SIMON & SCHUSTER and colophon are registered trademarks of Simon & Schuster, Inc.

The photographs of Michael Groover and Paula Deen on their wedding day are courtesy
of Photography by Lori. All other photographs are from the collection of the author.

For information about special discounts for bulk purchases,
please contact Simon & Schuster Special Sales at
1-866-506-1949 or business@simonandschuster.com.

The Simon & Schuster Speakers Bureau can bring authors
to your live event. For more information or to book an event,
contact the Simon & Schuster Speakers Bureau at
1-866-248-3049 or visit our website at www.simonspeakers.com.

Designed by Jessica Shatan Heslin / Studio Shatan, Inc.

Manufactured in the United States of America

10   9   8   7   6   5   4   3   2   1

Library of Congress Cataloging-in-Publication Data
Groover, Michael.
  My delicious life with Paula Deen / by Michael Groover with Sherry Suib Cohen.
      p.   cm.
    1. Cookery—Miscellanea.   2. Groover, Michael, 1955–   3. Deen, Paula H., 1947–
4. Spouses—Biography.   I. Cohen, Sherry Suib.   II. Title.
TX652.G7493 2009
641.5092—dc
[B]   2009031554

ISBN 978-1-4767-4735-4

This book is for my darling Paula,

my soul mate, my friend, my lover.

When you opened up your arms to me,

you opened up the world to me.

You are my everything.

ACKNOWLEDGMENTS

I give thanks for Paula Deen, always and ever, my Paula.

My warm appreciation to Sherry Suib Cohen, my friend and collaborator, who has come to love the language, the loyalties, and the unique ways of the South, as well as to her husband, Larry Cohen, who shares my abiding love of the sea.

My brothers, Henry B. Groover III, known as Father Hank, and Joseph Nicholas Groover, known as Nick, have always been there for me, and I will love and be grateful to them for all my life. Hank is a talented Southern and former tugboat cook, and I thank him for all his assistance with my recipes and our childhood memories. I'm also indebted to Nick's wife, Jodi Groover, for a great recipe and for her constant warmth. Their children, Jordan and Lauren, are just terrific.

To my own much-admired son, Anthony Groover, my beautiful daughter, Michelle Reed, and her husband, Daniel Reed—I cherish you three more than I can ever say. A special thank-you to Anthony's darling girlfriend, Jennifer Moesch.

More love and grateful recognition goes to Paula's kids, who I think of as my own—Bobby Deen, Jamie Deen and his wife, Brooke Deen, and their jackpot of a son—our grandson, little Jack Deen.

How lucky was I to find not only Paula but her fabulous extended family: my incredible brother-in-law, Earl Hiers Jr., otherwise known as the famous Bubba, and his great kids, Jay and Corrie, and Corrie's new fiancé, Brian Rooks. Paula's aunt Peggy Ort doesn't miss a trick and is an integral part of everything we do. Paula's cousin Don Hiers and his wife, Darlene, will always be part of my heart.

Never-ending thanks go to our great professional team, which consists of Paula's personal assistant and right-hand man, the incomparable Brandon Branch; her beloved agent, Barry Weiner, who is never wrong; her ever-attentive accountant, Karl Schumacher, CFO; and her treasured, indispensable staff, Theresa Feuger, Michelle White, and my friend and Paula's guardian angel, Hollis Johnson. The rest of wonderful Team Paula includes Jamie Cribbs, Courtney Fix, Sarah Meighan, and Cassie Aimar: we love them all.

We both owe the world to Nancy Assuncao, Paula's intuitive and powerful public relations expert.

So much gratitude goes to the wild and brilliantly talented producer Gordon Elliott, who first saw the true star qualities of Paula Deen.

My literary family is responsible for this book, a dream come true, especially Janis Donnaud, my loyal and wise literary agent. Our Simon & Schuster family is the heart of the best publishing: Sydny Miner is the VP and senior editor who understands language so well (even our Southern dialect) and gave *My Delicious Life with Paula Deen* the utmost diligence and care. I know there are some bawdy-ish words and jokes she'd have banished but for her determination to allow my own real self to speak in my own real stories. Michelle Rorke, assistant editor, could not have been more professional and helpful. Other brilliant S&S people who worked on this book are

Nancy Singer and Jessica Shatan Heslin, who were responsible for the impressive interior design; Sybil Pincus, senior production editor, and Libby Kessman, copy editor extraordinaire; and Brian Ulicky, the publicity director, who uses his wit and impressive contacts to bring notice of *My Delicious Life* to the world.

To David Rosenthal, Simon & Schuster's publisher, who leads our whole book team, so much gratitude.

Deep thanks to the Food Network, which has adopted me as its grizzled, seafarin' son—because Paula would have it no other way.

Thank you to Shara Arnofsky for a really great idea, and to the creative Shân Willis of Wordsmithery for transcribing my spoken stories and thoughts into written words for this book. Sherry's literary agent, Mel Berger of the William Morris Agency, is a nonpareil.

Finally, for the memories of my saintly momma, Carmel Register Groover, and my marvelous daddy, Henry B. Groover Jr.—may God rest their souls—I give my lifelong gratitude.

Without my family and extended family, this book would not have happened.

Last, but not least, my eternal thankfulness to Sam and Otis. They know why.

CONTENTS

FOREWORD

by Paula Deen

Hi y'all,

Listen: I felt like it was my place to introduce the world to my Captain Michael Groover. And, of course, I also felt that maybe I need to do a little groundwork to help prepare y'all for that meetin'.

Michael's not old—he's only fifty-three, but he's a true ol' Southern river boy. Now, ol' Southern river boys may be a little rough around the edges, and so, I want you to be prepared. His language and his jokes may be a little like the water we live on—salty—and he can also be rough and gruff and bawdy at times.

But when times are hard, Michael Groover will make the best friend that y'all could ever hope to have in this world.

I fell in love with this salty sea captain. And I guess you could say the first thing I fell in love with was his sense of humor: very dry and very witty.

Michael Groover made me laugh and he makes me laugh every day of my life. He brought laughter and joy into a personal life that was very sad at the time I met him. I will always love him for that.

So get ready to meet this rough-gruff-on-the-outside man who's a teddy bear on the inside. I think by the time you finish this book, you'll know why I fell in love with Captain Michael and why I will love the man until the day I die.

MY
Delicious Life
WITH
Paula Deen

PROLOGUE

Miss Paula Deen came into my life bringin' blue eyes, beamin' smiles, balance, and butter—no end of the butter.

All of those great things arrived in one pretty package and standin' on the most gorgeous legs you ever did see.

But among all the kick-ass gifts that Paula gave me, a beautiful balance was the most life changing. Up until we married, my days were spent on local waters, lonely but livin' and workin' at the job of my dreams as a harbor pilot in Savannah, Georgia. It was a wonderful life and all I ever wanted, all I needed.

I thought.

What I never gave a thought to was seein' the Eiffel Tower, zippin' through a jungle along a sturdy sky-high cable, wonderin' how it was to have people ask *me* for my autograph, bein' the owner of a classic, bright orange, muscle car, hangin'out with Billy Joel, havin' close friends of every race, religion, and sexual persuasion the good Lord made, marryin' and cookin' on television with one of the most famous television cooks on the planet, and then, goin' home with her and curlin' up in our giant bed for a little inspired romance. Inspired by the cook, I might add. That fabulous, adorable cook.

Paula brought the most vivid colors you can imagine into a happy life of mostly soft ocean blues and cloudy-day grays bordered by sameness. The eggy yellows, steaming reds, hot oranges, peacock blues of the whole world suddenly opened up to me. Fame and fortune and good fellowship came to balance a very quiet life. Nothing has ever been the same again.

There have been some bumps, of course. What couple gets through life without a bump now and then? There were also some pretty damn embarrassin' moments, and I'm thankin' the Lord that, knowin' Paula, there weren't a whole lot more.

So, if you've ever wondered how delicious it is to marry a celebrated but also good, funny, smart, and sassy person whom the whole world loves, climb aboard with me. There's some interestin' sailin' ahead.

1

Life Before Paula

*I didn't work my way to the top o' the food chain to eat carrots.
In fact, if someone offers me a salad, I say, "That's what my
food eats—salads."*

I was born Michael Anthony Groover on December 13, 1955. I
shared my first home with my saint of a mother, Carmel Register
Groover, and my father, Henry B. Groover Jr., known as Big Henry.
Rounding out the family in my home were my eighteen-month-
older brother, Henry B. Groover III, or Hank; my little brother, Joseph Nicholas Groover, or Nick; and my maternal grandfather
Joseph Anthony Register, or Poppa, possibly one of the hardest
workers I'll ever know.

My childhood days were filled with heat and bugs, heat and bugs,
heat and bugs and, I think, for the grown-ups, a little beer to take
their minds off the heat and bugs. We kids had no air conditioner so
we created our own breezes on bikes or boats, swatting at the horse-
flies much of the time. For our family, the four seasons were almost

summer, summer, still summer, and Christmas. The first cool snap, in fact, was in November, when the temperature fell to below seventy degrees, also known as good stew weather.

Speakin' of stew, we cooked anything we could shoot, fish up, or catch. With all due respect to the animal rights folks, I surely believed then and now that there's room in this world for all God's creatures—right on my plate next to my mashed potatoes.

That first house was a small four-room, one-bath building with two screened porches, built by my paternal grandfather Pop and his children. The tiny house sat on a bend on Turner's Creek with a breathtaking westerly view; I think it's the most beautiful land on Savannah's Wilmington Island. Within a kid's reach there was hangin' moss, palm trees, and the most fragrant bloomin' wild roses, magnolias, and dogwood you ever did see. As a member of the third generation of Groovers on Wilmington Island, I have witnessed some of the most stunning sunsets known to man or woman.

We might have had a shortage of rooms but we surely had an abundance of love. During my wakin' hours I stayed outdoors. Sometimes it got real hot and dry, but we didn't care since 100 degrees Fahrenheit is considered only a bit warm in Savannah. It was just a great place, our private stompin' grounds, and it was like having a seaside country of our own.

Without a doubt we weren't rich, but we really didn't know we weren't rich. My father worked with the railroad and he made a good, honest livin'. No tellin' how many kids lived on Wilmington Island my daddy taught to swim—had to be at least a hundred. He worked hard and he spent most of his money on us. My folks never lived extravagantly or above their means; and we kids never lived above our raising. My brother Hank, who's a priest today, and I had bunk beds. In those days, you didn't put the old folks away in an old-age home, so my grandfather stayed in the bed adjacent to us right in our room. And we had to walk through my mother and father's bedroom to get to our bedroom.

When my younger brother Nick was born, Hank and I moved to the porch and lived there eight months out of the year. When nights got real cold, in the mid-thirties in January, we reluctantly came back inside.

We had a barn to house our animals; they kept us busy and taught us responsibility. We had ponies, horses, cows, pigs, turkeys, chickens, geese, and ducks. We also raised English bulldogs.

We had to feed and water the animals twice daily; we collected eggs, milked the cows, cleaned up the manure, doctored the sick, and separated the bullies. As my brother Hank says, it taught us respect for nature.

We'd hear people sayin', "Oh, we had this calf and then my father had him butchered and it was the worst day of my life and I'll never eat ground beef again." Well, as Hank points out, we also had a calf and it was no accident we named him T-Bone. We knew where he was eventually goin'—that's nature and that's how we existed on the farm. If the chickens weren't layin' they went in the pot. We cared for our animals and made sure they had veterinary care and food and water, but we also knew the chickens didn't volunteer for the colonel's bucket.

Outside our window, there was a show every day and night in the creek. I remember one midnight my mother was so frightened because for a couple of days, she'd been thinkin' she heard someone on the porch, breathing heavy. She was sure the intruder was lookin' in the bedroom window but she was reluctant to tell my dad because she knew he'd go outside and really hurt that person and end up in jail. Finally, she couldn't stand it, woke him up, yellin', "Henry, Henry there's someone outside, breathin' heavy right out our window!" My daddy jumped up, ran outside, and listened.

It was the dolphins swimmin' up and down the creek, arching and jumping as they surfaced. Dolphins are mammals; they have to breathe air and that's what they were doin'—makin' a *psh-psh-psh* breathing sound as they leaped. They're silvery gray—almost the color of a Weimaraner dog—and they move like ballerinas. It's an amazing thing to see—they are so graceful when they leap, and they never touch each other, even though there may be six or eight of them leaping at a time. That's what my momma was hearing—those dolphins breathin' at their play. Although of course she'd seen them in the day, somehow she'd never heard them in the middle of the night and she didn't recognize the sound. As a child, I saw them swim ahead of the bow of my boat when I was out exploring the waters.

On our property was a tiny house that actually had several uses. It was, at different times, used for storage, a dog kennel, and—most important—our kids' clubhouse. We called it the Bonehead House. When we were about twelve and thirteen, the guys and I would hunt for turtle and horse skulls on the beaches and we'd nail them up on the Bonehead House to scare away the girls. When I was sixteen, I moved into the Bonehead House full-time.

At that point, my brothers and I decided we kinda liked girls, and we took down those skulls. I guess you could say the house should really have been called the Underage Club because my brothers and I were definitely underage, but I looked old enough to go buy Miller Pony beers. They don't make 'em anymore but they were these little short beers that you could swallow in one gulp. Our refrigerator had nothing but Pony beers in it.

I'm sorry to tell y'all we also kept a small stash of pot hidden on the grounds; the girls thought it was cool. Even though our clubhouse was only about fifty feet from where our parents slept, it was very private because Momma and Daddy went to sleep with the birds right after the six o'clock news and woke up with the birds at dawn. My father was a very strict disciplinarian and if there was any-thing I feared, it was him. He used to say, "I'll ask you once, I'll tell you twice, the next time won't be so nice."

I hate to think what would have happened if he ever opened that refrigerator.

Actually, it was pretty funny: Poppa, who lived with us, had his own bigger place on the south end of Wilmington Island. That big-ger place stayed empty. He *wanted* to live with us and we wanted him to live with us. I've always been glad he did. Why? Well, he was prob-ably the hardest worker I've ever met, always fiddling and workin' in the yard: He had rootin' boxes, he'd forever be planting stuff in beds. So, we always had a garden, probably an acre. We would plant toma-toes an' peas an' onions with our granddaddy, and we never knew what grand thing would be bursting out of the earth next.

We always had enough, but *just* enough. If Daddy's check from the railroad hadn't come in yet, my brothers and I would go out in the boat and catch shrimp or oysters so the family could eat. Some-times we'd pick up the pears that fell from our tree and we'd trade them with the grocer for a roast. What Daddy made and how we spent it was never a secret.

We each had a wish list of what we wanted to buy that week, but there were the necessities and if Daddy's check hadn't come in, we would negotiate. Actually, as Hank remembers, it allowed us to be generous. If one person needed shoes badly, the other would say, "Well, I'll wait on that jacket I want; you getcher shoes this month" (although shoes were nothing we were ever real crazy about).

Our childhood flew by. One minute we were fixin' to catch us some snakes (there are 5,000 types of snakes and 4,998 of them live in Georgia) and the next minute we got interested in girls.

My momma was a fabulous cook—I don't know who woulda liked Paula more, my momma or my daddy, because my daddy definitely liked to eat. Daddy liked strong women; he sure would have admired Paula Deen, and my momma and Paula coulda cooked together and traded recipes. It is a damn shame they never knew her.

My daddy also loved the sea, and I guess that and bein' raised on the water is where I got my lifelong love of the sea. Seems like every night when my daddy went to bed, he had a "dream book" with him. That's what he called his treasured boating magazines. He wanted to buy a shrimp boat or a serious fishin' boat but he never could afford it. Toward the end of his life, we did buy a small shrimp boat but never did a whole lot with it.

Right on our creek lived several people who also went on to maritime careers like me, like my younger brother Nick, who's a river pilot. Captain Judy, our neighbor who still lives right one door down, is a charter boat captain. Like me, they never left the place we were raised up in. Pretty powerful pull, these Savannah waters.

I knew early on that I had to raise my own kids, when I had 'em, on the water, because you can always keep kids busy there. They can go fishin' or skiing or crabbin' or just go to the beaches. They can go shark tooth huntin' or just ridin' out in the boat. My momma used to say, "An idle mind is the devil's workshop," so we weren't allowed to be idle: You can't stand on the street corner and buy drugs if you're not idly standin' on the street corner. So all of us stayed damn busy during my comin' up. Even if you yourself didn't have a boat, one of your friends would come by and say, "You wanna go skiin'?" or "You wanna go fishin'?" or "You wanna go just to the islands?"

We always owned a motor and a very small boat; my brother Hank and I were either hangin' out at the dock or investigatin' every river, beach, and island near our house. Georgia has barrier islands and we always loved to explore them. It was better than any Harry Potter adventure, believe me. Hank and I have gone up every creek there is around, just to see what was at the end of the creek and what was around the next corner. We fished, crabbed, shrimped, water-skied, and hunted for sharks' teeth and marsh hens. We had a network of friends who lived on the water. Long before any of us got a driver's license and a car, we had boats; they were our primary means of transportation. When we were not boatin' or swimmin', there were motorcycles and horses and miles of trails and woods to enjoy.

Most of us had girlfriends by the time we got to be teenagers. There were lots of girls who lived on Wilmington Island. Some were good girls and some were bad girls and we loved them all. Further on down the street, there was a family my momma didn't like. I can remember my momma tellin' me, "Don't go to these people's house—they're bad news, they're just very bad news."

Naturally, that's just where I would go, a lot. There was this one girl, and again, she wasn't really a bad girl. We would play Spin the Bottle and Post Office, she and I. I couldn'ta been ten years old when she said, "I'll show you mine if you show me yours."

I said okay. So I did and she did. An' it just freaked me out.

I was down there another time—against my mother's wishes—and a kid from another neighborhood came over and he was climbin' in the tree. One of the boys walked out there and says, "Get out of my tree."

The other kid says, "No, I'm not gettin' out o' yer tree, 'cause it's not yer tree."

Then the boy goes inside his house, gets a .22 rifle, an' shoots the other kid in the stomach.

I ran so fast, I mean, I just knew my mother was gonna kill me if the police woulda' interviewed me and she'd known I was there. So I took off runnin'. Never went back there again.

Once, a friend an' I were diggin' an underground fort in the side of this ditch an' we would shore it up as we went along. We were puttin' in four-by-fours and plywood while we were tunnelin' through it and my mother said, "Don't go back there. Y'all gonna get in trouble there. Do not go in there, somethin's gonna happen to y'all."

I didn't go back to the fort after she said that, and soon after, it collapsed and suffocated the kid from down the street, may God rest his soul.

So life taught us some hard lessons and I was also startin' to get the idea to listen to my mother. Living on the sea made us like little wild things in some ways, but it also gave us respect for the land and the water and for each other. I knew I never wanted to be far from the water. I certainly didn't want to live next door to a one-hundred-unit condominium community, which I laughingly called the "Projects."

Till Paula.

I was raised Catholic: My mother was very religious, and my father was a convert to Catholicism—he'd been born a Lutheran. Hank and I were both altar boys, and durin' Lent, we would serve Mass every mornin' before school.

When we were in grade school, we lived about five miles or so from the Catholic school but we didn't like to ride the regular bus, which we called "the Rattletrap." Miss Mulligan was the dear old lady who used to run the bus and she was as strict as a drill sergeant. Worst of all, she made us say the rosary every day on the bus, so Hank and I would hide in a ditch until the bus went by and then we'd thumb a ride. Every mornin' the same nurse would pick us up and drop us off at school. We loved that nurse: We got to school earlier, we got to play longer, and we didn't have to say the rosary. What's more, the nurse's car was much more comfortable than the Rattletrap. We pulled that off for four or five months until one day in the grocery store my mother happened to meet the lady who gave us the rides. She said to my momma, "Mrs. Groover, I have to tell you, you have the two most polite children I ever met."

Momma said, "Well, thank you. Does the heart good to hear that, but where do you know my boys from?"

The nurse said, "I give them a ride every morning to school."

Momma said, "No, you're mistaken. My sons ride the bus to school."

"No," said the nurse, "I give them a ride every mornin' in my car."

At dinner, Momma confronted us and we had to tell her the whole story.

"Don't tell me that," Momma said. "I been payin' five dollars extra a month for y'all to ride the school bus. So, please ride the bus."

So we did.

Then I went to a military high school run by the Benedictine monks. I wasn't born with this beard—I grew it after the military high school where I had to shave every day. Hank continued at Catholic colleges because he was college material. Frankly, I was tired of school after high school—the sea was waiting for me, you might say, but Hank went to college for sixteen years. My brother who was not tired o' school made up for me who was.

I can remember in school they would ask us kids what we wanted to be when we grew up. Most kids had not a clue what they wanted to be—maybe a fireman or a policeman or a circus guy. But Hank from the time he was five years old would always say priest. I always said boat captain.

Well, I followed my dream and when I graduated at seventeen in 1973 from the Benedictine Military School, I got a job as a deckhand on a tugboat by lyin' about my age and tellin' them I was already eighteen. I always felt like a bad day on the water is a lot better than a good day on shore. My favorite captain was a great guy named

Gerald Missroon and he trained me how to run a tugboat. He was real passionate about doin' everything the right way: No compromise—you did it right the first time. He also taught me a lot about how to treat people.

Well, one night, goin' home, he had burned the candle on both ends. His car hit a tree and he got killed. He was a single dad with three boys and losin' him broke my heart. I became captain that very day.

David Missroon, his son, eventually became my deckhand and I, in turn, trained David in the same skills his dad taught me. I also trained Gerald's youngest son, Kevin, to be a captain. Well, David also became a captain and, I'm proud to say, a docking pilot. Today, Anthony, my son, is David's first mate on the tugboat the *Edward J. Moran*. Life's funny. In a roundabout way David's dad is teaching my son. I like to think that Gerald is looking down on all of us with a huge smile, saying, "Good job, guys!"

I've been on tugboats ever since; it's practically my religion. It's never a chore to go to work—it's pure happiness. I think workin' a job you hate is how addictions start: I know I'd have to have a double happy hour every day if I worked eight hours at something I didn't like. I'd definitely have to drown my sorrows.

I came up at about the time of the Vietnam War. None of us were really exposed to the civil rights movement; I guess you could say we were sheltered. My parents were very kind people and I don't think they ever even noticed that the three black families who lived on Wilmington Island were indeed black. I think in my grandaddy's time, people were afraid of anything different and bein' black was real different then. If my grandaddy saw a black person wandering around on Wilmington Island, he'd assume the person must have escaped from a nearby chain gang.

But when it came to my raising, it was another story. Then there were quite a few strong black families on the island, who worked real hard and whose kids often went to college. Boats were in all our blood. Sam and Lizzie were one such couple; we kids would go over there and trade chickens with them. Under the bridge lived Miz Missouri White who was black, and Daddy would always pick her up and give her a ride to wherever she was goin'. Once I was with him and I remember she said she had twenty-two young'uns and Daddy asked her if they were all by the same father. She said, "Oh, Lord, no."

Southern people allow for incredible individual diversity and eccentric behavior, as my brother Hank points out. I remember very well how Missouri White would dance for pennies in front of Mitchell's Log Cabin, our local gas station, bar, and grocery. When she got tired, Daddy or one of us—whoever happened to be standin' there—would put her in our truck to drive her back to her home. Miz Missouri always had a ride home.

The South has a code of manners. If you knew so and so was what others might call the village idiot, you'd still never laugh at him, or pass him in the street without sayin' good mornin' or good evenin'. One of us would always be pickin' up ol' Mrs. Houston when she got lost and bring her to our home where Momma would wrap her legs in Ace bandages and tend to her varicose veins before we gave her a ride home.

When I was a little older, I had a black friend named Benny; we worked on the tugboats together. Benny was a big guy, 350 pounds and six foot four. He had eight girlfriends and a wife. He would go visit each of them separately.

One day I asked Benny, "Benny, do you plan to buy a house?"

He said, "No, I don't wanna house."

I said, "Well, do you have a savings account?"

He said, "No."

I said, "Well, then, let's get you a savings account."

So Benny and I opened a savings account in his name. The bank told me we both had to sign for Benny to get money out of the savings account; I didn't know why, but we did that. We saved, like, six thousand dollars for him and then our plan was for him to buy a house. I told him if he went into a white neighborhood where blacks had already moved in, he could get a better house, cheaper, because the white people seemed to want to move out when the black folks moved in. It was the truth, that's all I knew.

One day Benny came to me and said, "Gimme my money. I want my money."

I said, "Well, you were savin' for the house."

He said, "Well, I don't care. I want my money."

So I signed and gave him his money, and that weekend he spent the whole six thousand dollars.

You know, I felt like he was just learnin' about money and when the numbers got too big and he saw he had six thousand dollars, he needed to spend it. I was disappointed and I told him.

Benny said, "You know, Michael, if you were black for one day on payday, you would not wanna be white again."

I didn't really understand what he meant. Now I think he meant that he could party that strong on payday, stronger than any white man, and have a good time the likes of which white people couldn't understand.

Still, Benny and I were good friends.

Sometimes we would go to River Street and if the bar we went into was crowded, we ended up as unpaid bouncers for that bar. They would pay us in beer to break up fights and throw the bad guys out. Once a guy's wife came in, hoppin' mad. He was three sheets to the wind but that didn't stop him from saying, quick as you please, "I knew if I stayed in this bar long enough, I'd catch you comin' in here!"

Sometimes Benny an' I would start a fake fight; it would look like a kind of a race fight. People would jump up and leave, then we would sit at their table and drink. That's about how much I thought about race relations back then—the fun Benny and I had staging those fake fights.

After Benny spent his money, I told myself, *Well, you know, you can't teach other people to think the way you think. Everybody has different goals, and his goal is to work, get paid, get high, and party hard.*

I saw Benny several times over the years, and he did drugs till the day he died. I would sometimes bring him to his kidney dialysis. But he was a really good-hearted guy and a victim of the worst times in the South because he was probably taught that the best fun he could hope to enjoy was to have a buzz from drugs or alcohol. He felt he didn't have much to look forward to, I guess. That house was never gonna happen, he thought, no matter how much he saved.

Benny passed away recently. I went to his funeral; I was the only white person there. If I wouldna' been as obvious as a turd in a punchbowl, I woulda got up and left when the preacher said, "Well, we cannot save or change Brother Benjamin now, but we're gonna try to save y'all."

He preached an' preached an' preached to us, but I was feelin' *so* pissed. There was a whole lot good he could have said about Brother Benjamin but he chose not to. I wanted to get out, but I couldn't get up and leave.

Without a doubt, I felt sorry for what happened to my pal Benny. But everybody *does* have different goals. My goal was to buy a house, get married, and raise kids. Benny had a wife and eight girl-friends. Look, I think he enjoyed his life, but he never had a chance to see a bigger picture beyond those women.

The job I have today, which I got way before I met Paula, is the culmination of everything I learned and wanted in my childhood. It's an important job in which I've built enormous self-esteem. That's the name of the game, isn't it—to do well at something you love and to have others respect you for it. I have to admit, though, as steady as I feel about my work, sometimes it's hard to play second fiddle to Paula's fame, although playing second fiddle to Paula ain't such a bad gig. It's not that I need top billing, it's just that I've worked so hard at climbing to the top of my own field that I want others to understand what I do. Paula understands what it means to me, and I love her for that.

I'm a dockin' pilot, or as some call 'em, harbor pilot. That's pretty much the top tier where I work. In this business, you start off as a relief deckhand, then you become a deckhand, then a relief captain, then a captain, then a relief dockin' pilot, and finally, a full-time dockin' pilot.

We have a two-pilot system here on the East Coast. We have river pilots, who bring a ship up the river an' keep the ship in the channel until they get in close proximity of the dock. Then the dockin' pilot goes aboard and relieves the river pilot; the dockin' pilot uses assist boats, which are tugboats, to help turn the ship around and dock it or bring it safely to the pier. That's not so easy with boats the length of three football fields, even though my friend Buckethead some-times says I'm a high-price valet parking attendant for ships. Those tugboats connect to the ships with large ropes, but the tugs are so powerful, they can easily part or even break the ropes, and then the ropes can hurl back like a slingshot; they could kill you if you're not careful and experienced.

Oh, without a doubt I was *proud* when I became a full dockin' pilot. It meant a lot to me, and I accomplished it pretty fast. It's a lotta hours, a lotta dedication, a lotta responsibility, but it's a very lucrative job. If you're not passionate about it, though, you'll find a heap to complain about—the long and late hours, the missed Easters and Christmases, the missed recitals and baseball and football games, the missed dinners with your wife. The good part was that when my kids were little, I could work a week off and a week on, so I could often pick the kids up at school and be around at different times of the day when most daddies were never seen.

Here's the dockin' pilot's routine: I give commands to the quartermaster of the big ship who's at the speed throttle. I also give commands to the helmsman, who steers. Every time I give a command, it's repeated by the captain, repeated by the helmsman or quartermaster, and then repeated back to me so I can be sure it's the exact command I gave.

Then I give all the tugboats my commands. I communicate with the tugs separately—normally there are two but there may be as many as four of them on a job—and I'm telling one tug to push forward and another to go in reverse. They answer my commands with special whistles to inform me they've received my orders. It gets very complicated but the idea is to lay that big river ship baby safely, neatly, and nicely to the pier.

My son Anthony and my son-in-law Daniel are mates on the tugboats. My brother Nick is a river pilot and he brings the ship up the river. I turn it around and dock it. All the while, our brother Hank, who is the priest, is prayin' that we don't hit anything. It's a family business, you could say.

My job is precise and exacting work. All this time I'm givin' commands, the currents and the winds are moving the vessels along with the engine and I have to adjust for that as well. The work is intense. Your concentration must be sharp and unwavering. The stakes are high. A mistake can seriously damage the vessel, the dock, and people.

You know, the largest ships that come in at Savannah are the LNG—the liquid natural gas tankers. They are about 950 feet long and 150 feet wide. They're big girls. Savannah's the fourth largest container port in the country. Most of our ships are container ships. The largest is 965 by 106 feet. That's what you call a Panamax ship, the largest ship they can get through the Panama Canal. This is a big part of what I do, what I am. This is what I was before Paula and what I brought to our lives today.

When I was little more than a teenager, I married too young. It started off well, we had two incredible children, but then our ship went off course and foundered. After years of trying to bring the marriage back to an even keel, we both realized it wasn't going to work.

We divorced.

The best things that came from my first marriage were my two beloved children, Michelle and Anthony. The worst things that came were sadness and disagreements and misunderstandin's. I learned to pull back and withdraw emotionally when I was hurt.

I'm not going to say anything bad about my ex-wife because I don't want to hurt her or our kids. This book is about me and Paula and not meant to point out the flaws in my first marriage. Suffice it to mention that the marriage was good when it was good and bad when it was bad.

My ex-wife's personality just baffled me and I'm sure she would have a lot to say about my own charming personality. People make mistakes, and we both did.

So, there we were. I was living alone with my black Labrador,

Cody, and my kids, who thrived and grew. I really tried hard and you know what? I wasn't so bad as a single daddy. But my friends said, "Mike, you just have to get out. You'll never meet anyone stayin' in that house on that dead-end road. No one even comes down that road."

But then a loopy, white-haired gal with sky blue eyes came rushin'—not exactly down the road—but around a fence and into my backyard. Before I was fifty years of age, this wild hurricane blew into my life.

Her name was Paula Deen.

Captain's Deviled Crabs
My Mother Carmel's Recipe

A perfect romantic dinner with leftovers.

PREP TIME: About 40 minutes, including cooking time
MAKES: About 6 filled crab shell servings

1 stick plus 6 tablespoons butter
1 cup finely chopped onion
½ cup finely chopped celery
½ cup finely chopped bell pepper, any color
1 tablespoon chopped parsley
½ teaspoon dried thyme
2 tablespoons *real* mayonnaise
Couple of shots of hot sauce, *optional*
1 teaspoon salt
¼ teaspoon black pepper
¼ teaspoon white pepper
¼ teaspoon cayenne pepper
2 well-beaten eggs
1½ pounds fresh lump crabmeat
¾ cup crushed Ritz or saltine crackers
Paprika

Preheat the oven to 350°F.

Begin by meltin' a stick of butter in a medium-sized skillet and sauté the onions, celery, bell pepper, parsley, and thyme until the vegetables are just tender, 5 to 7 minutes. Do not let your butter burn. When the vegetables are tender, place the contents of skillet into a large mixin' bowl. Add the mayo, hot sauce, salt, and black, white, and cayenne peppers and lightly toss together. The contents of the mixin' bowl should be cool enough now to add the eggs. Stir gently. Then in goes the crab-meat. Try not to stir too vigorously, because y'all want nice, unbroken lumps of crabmeat. Now add the cracker crumbs a little at a time. Y'all want just enough cracker crumbs to help hold this mixture together nice and firm, but you do not want it bready. The dominant flavor should be crab! If you're usin' fresh crabs, clean the back shells of the crabs with a vegetable brush and place the deviled crab mixture in them. They now have foil crab shell things at the grocery store or you can use a ramekin. If I'm usin' fresh crabs, I'll use the shells from the crabs I just picked out.

Place the fillin' in the shells lightly—don't pack it down. Place the loaded shells on a cookie sheet, dot with the remaining butter, and sprinkle with a little paprika. Bake for 20 to 25 minutes, until light brown. ⚓

2

So, This Wild, White-Haired Gal Comes Rushin' into My Backyard

What do y'all call a cow with three legs?
   Lean beef
What do y'all call a cow with no legs?
   Ground beef
What do y'all call a bull playin' with himself?
   Beef stroganoff

When I first met Paula, I wasn't thinkin' of marriage. I'd recently come off a long and tough marriage, and I felt like I'd been rode hard and put up wet. I'd just given up on anything serious with any woman on the planet. I'd pretty much made a vow, matter of fact, that I didn't want to marry again and I'd be happy to live the rest of my life alone with my children.

Actually, I was just standin' around outside, mindin' my own damn business, in my own damn backyard. Fact is I'd been banned from smokin' in the house by my daughter, Michelle, and she'd made me go outside whenever tobacco was involved. Paula likes to tell this story a different way. She says that I was just hangin' out doin' nothin' like a crazy, old vagrant, but I was actually smokin' and talkin' on my cell phone. Then I noticed these two tiny, sorry-lookin' black-and-white dogs who were mighty busy poopin' all over my lawn.

Lessee, I don't want to give the wrong impression. You know, I was definitely interested in meetin' different people, and I sure hadn't given up on the women part of people, but as I mentioned, gettin' serious with a woman and certainly marriage was out of the question.

When I had a woman friend over to my house, I didn't even like to see an overnight bag. No one was gonna stay there that long. My idea of a long-term relationship was about an hour. Actually that might be stretchin' it a little.

I particularly liked women over forty. As one poet pal put it, "They don't swell, they don't tell, and they're grateful as hell." Actually, I liked all women, but the ones who were older seemed to like me more.

So when I met this white-haired gal who come galomphin' onto my property yellin' her dogs had gotten loose, I got interested. Probably the initial thing that really had me excited about Paula—the first thing that caught my attention anyway—was her eyes. God, they were this gorgeous, deep, early mornin,' sparklin' sea blue eyes—I'd never seen anyone with eyes like that. And her enthusiasm and energy were contagious. She didn't know me from a hole in the wall, but she was talkin' fast and grinnin' and apologizin' for the dogs—and, well, I could hardly catch my breath: She was so *all* woman.

Where had she come from? Unfortunately, I knew. They'd built some pretty fancy condos right next to my house, the one in which I'd raised my kids, and Paula lived in those condos I call the Projects. When they started buildin' them, my brother Nick and I had hired a lawyer to try to stop the Projects, or at least to make 'em less obnoxious. They'd already had to stop at my house because I wouldn't sell 'em my lot. So we compromised: The builders put up fewer units and they built an eight-foot-tall stucco fence so I wouldn't have to look at the buildings. That was where Paula had chased her runaway dogs—around the condo wall to my house.

I'd never seen Paula before in person, but I remembered where I'd seen her picture: I recognized her from her photograph in the cookbooks she'd written. I'd even given one of them as a gift; we are all into Southern cookin' around here in Savannah.

Years later, Paula told me that if I'd continued to look as scraggly as I did that first day, with my beard long and unkempt, she probably woulda never married me. I told her that if she really looked like Aunt Bee from Mayberry like she did on the cover of *The Lady & Sons, Too!*, her second cookbook, there's a good chance I woulda never married her either.

Anyway, so I'm in the backyard, and these two little dogs come up to me. I'm a huge animal lover—me and the dogs hit it off right away, way before Paula came around. So I was pettin' the dogs, playin' with 'em, and Paula ran up and said, "I'm *so* sorry."

She was wearin' jeans, an apron, and a baseball cap over her gray hair and was screamin' "Stop! Sit! Stop!" to the dogs, who paid not a bit of attention to her. I noticed her accent. I really liked it; it was an interesting accent, a little more Southern than most. You don't have to go too far out of Savannah and you'll get a little more of a twang, and when you go to southwest Georgia, it's even more pronounced. Or unpronounced. Or somethin'. They add more syllables. She looked me right in my eyes with those incredible piercing blue eyes and said she was sorry that the dogs were poopin' in the yard and she would clean it up. I remember she mentioned she was writin' a new cookbook and didn't get out much because she was so busy. To be neighborly, I said, "Well, maybe you ought to take a break one day and we could go out for a drink or somethin'."

"Yeah, okay," she said. She didn't seem too enthusiastic and apologized again for the poopin' dogs.

I said, "That's okay, I like dogs. It's people I'm not sure about." What I meant by that is in two minutes you can mainly tell whether you can trust a dog or not, whether they'll bite you or not. And sometimes, with people, it'll take a lifetime and you still don't know if they'll bite you.

Naturally, Paula didn't understand where I was comin' from with that brilliant pickup line, so she grabbed the dogs and took off runnin', thinkin' I was a nut. And since I wasn't, I was a little disappointed she'd left.

I thought I'd never see her again, so I didn't give it another minute's thought and went back to my smokin'. Later on in the week, I happened to mention to my brother Nick that this zany woman who I thought lived over in the Projects and was writin' a cookbook had popped onto my land. He said he thought a lady from town who owned a restaurant—he'd eaten there and liked it—lived next door to me. I told him I thought that might be the woman with the incontinent dogs, but I wasn't sure.

Probably two weeks later, I was out smokin' in my yard again and Paula shows up chasin' the dogs again! And naturally the dogs and I had already said our hellos—we're buddies by this time. Paula ran up, same thing. "Well, I'm sorry my dogs are poopin' in your backyard again," she said. "If you have a bag or somethin', I can clean it up. Please let me."

"It's okay," I said.

Then, makin' conversation, Paula asked me how long I'd lived there and this time she also asked if I knew anything about boats. Then, the deal closer for me—she told me she had a new boat. She said she'd just bought this boat. She knew how to operate the CD player real well, but could I possibly show her how to crank the boat itself up?

Well, askin' me if I know anything about boats is like askin' Paula Deen if she knows how to cook chicken. You know, I've never had a real job on land. I been out workin' on crab boats, snapper boats, any kind of boat you can imagine my whole life. I had the feeling she'd investigated me a little, although she'll deny that to her dyin' day. Anyway, she thought I knew enough about boats at least to teach her how to start hers up.

That's how the fire started.

It was more than intriguin' for me to meet an excellent cook who owned a restaurant, who was writin' a sweets cookbook, and who owned her own boat. My kinda woman. It'd been a coon's age since I met a woman like Ms. Paula Deen. Try never.

I said to myself, *Oh, gosh, this may be the perfect woman.*

Look—I figured I'd met somebody who not only has her own boat, but, you know, has a job (she mentioned her restaurant) and she *wants* to work and loves it. Well, that was the work ethic I have. You also could tell that this woman who burst onto my property was not a follower, she was a leader, afraid of very little. Every man dreams of havin' a partner who pulls in the same direction.

I was interested. Against my best judgment and against my carefully worked out plans, I found myself interested.

Did I mention that I thought she was gorgeous? And her legs—whoa.

So, since we were *real* neighbors, it was only right to make a date for me to go look at her boat. The next day, I went over to the Projects. I cranked the boat up while she watched carefully, went and fueled it up, and then we went for a ride. We went around Wassaw Sound, which is about three or four miles from where we lived. The water was very rough, and we were just jumpin' those waves and Paula was laughin' hysterically—you know that laugh. She just loved that boat ride and so did I. We headed back into the most beautiful sunset you ever saw, and pretty much, you know, life changed from that moment.

But I didn't know it then and she didn't either. I have to say, lookin' back, it was definitely not love at first sight for Paula, and maybe not for me either, but I was sure intrigued. I was powerfully intrigued. Later, she said the ride had seemed passionate for her, very sensual—that heavin' water and all that bangin' around on the boat. Turned her on, would you believe? Well, I didn't feel that kind of passion, having been on bangin' boats a whole lot, but as we walked back to her apartment, I was startin' to feel maybe what she felt on the boat.

It wasn't in the cards for that day.

But she invited me to come in, which I did. It was a little awkward. I think we both felt we needed an icebreaker, and then Paula showed me these crazy little books she had on the table. They were called *What if?* books and they asked you questions like *What if you had to spend a year on a desert island, what would you take with you?* Paula said she'd take a potato plant. I said I would take a boat so I could come get her and her potato plant and get us all home. Okay, they were kinda neat little books, but I probably got tired of *what if* a lot faster than she did.

So we began talking *what ifs* a little bit and, you know, she started flirtin' a little. What I didn't know was that Paula was comin' off a long, bad relationship and she was hungry for plain old niceness in a man, hungry for honesty.

I could do that, even though I didn't know her circumstances.

I told her I loved my motorcycle and she told me that she'd never ride on my motorcycle. Hmmmmmmm, not a great start. Later I learned her daddy was hurt in an accident, and she sure didn't like fast-moving vehicles. Then she said—I can't remember what prompted it—that she also would never kiss me. Paula's a great flirt, you know.

Later on, after the kiss finally happened, she admitted that all she wanted to find out was what was goin' on under my mustache and beard: did I, for instance, have teeth? She wasn't sure.

I told her I'd make the bet that eventually, she'd ride my motorcycle *and* give me a kiss. She said no way José.

It was time for a real date.

Turned out, after we talked a bit more, I found that Paula was on the Atkins diet—you know, the one where you can suck on a stick o' butter and eat bacon wrapped around your steak and still be on the diet. That should have given me my first clue about this woman.

So I said to myself, *If I asked her out, where do you take somebody like Paula Deen to eat? This is gonna be pretty tough.*

Then I had an idea.

"Would you like to go out to dinner?" I asked. "But there's one stipulation—it has to be your favorite place."

I felt pretty safe there, figurin' it would be prob'ly be the kinda frou-frou food I wasn't real crazy about. I was gonna let her pick so she'd be happy and think I was a sport. So she says, "Well, have you ever been to The Huddle House?"

As I said, Paula's my kind o' gal. The Huddle House is like a waffle place and they sell breakfasts mostly. Paula could get two eggs and a pound o' bacon and still stay on her Atkins diet. So I said, "Yes, I've been. Is that where you wanna go?"

She said, "Yes, I'd love to go there," and I said to myself, *Well, this won't be near as hard as I thought it was gonna be.*

So we went to the Huddle House, and did a lot more talkin' than eatin'. One of the first things that drew us together, and probably still does, is how we feel about our kids. So we talked a lot about them and it was growin' on me that this was an interestin' woman, a *real* woman, maybe someone that I'd been searchin' for all my life. And, oh gosh, that laugh of hers—it was infectious. Still is.

I always love to hear Paula laugh.

Even when we first met, she wasn't a nobody. She already had her own restaurant, The Lady & Sons, had published her second cookbook and was workin' on a third. After we married and she became *really* famous, someone introduced her as the Queen of Southern Cuisine. I said, "You know what you call the queen's husband, don't you? You call him the king."

It's good to be the king.

If you know anything about Paula, you know something about the South and its relationship to food. Even when someone's died, a Southerner knows that the best gesture of solace for someone's trouble is a plate of hot fried chicken, a big bowl of potato salad, and if there's a real crisis, a Southerner knows to add a gooey punkin' pie. Or a giant banana puddin'.

We were so happy, I couldn't believe it was happenin'. I remember early in our relationship going out on my buddy Billy Brown's big boat. We sat in a corner of the boat all night long, gigglin' and kissin' and actin' like dumb-ass teenagers. We hardly even noticed the boat was movin' or the scenery was passin' us by. Everybody left us alone; that's how obvious it was that we wanted to be alone.

We'd been datin' for about a month, laughin' and eatin' good all the while, when Paula told me she thought we should meet each other's families. I know Paula had talked to her boys a lot about me at the restaurant. It was time we actually met face-to-face.

Well, I just loved those two boys to death the minute we shook hands. I know that sounds odd coming from a guy, but there was something about her sons that reminded me of Anthony, and I wanted very much to get along with them. They seemed so natural and funny and real, just like their momma. Frankly, I was worried they would think I was tryin' to jump on the gravy train, that I had ulterior motives, that I didn't care for their mother for who she was but for what she had. The truth? I surely was beginning to love Paula Deen with all my heart. They say the way to a man's heart is through his stomach, and in my case without a doubt, it's true. Paula knew how to fill my stomach, and right along with it, my heart and my head. When I was single, I met girls who said they were in love with me but I knew why they said that: They wanted me to raise their children or they "loved" me for my salary. I know a lotta people hook up with women for different reasons, but I was not one of them; I was pretty much self-made, I never took anything from anyone, and I wanted Bobby and Jamie to know that.

You know what? I never *really* believed either one of 'em ever thought I was after their momma's newly made money, but I wanted to make sure they didn' think that I was there even for a short free ride.

Other problems were loomin' that smart me hadn't even thought of. They were comin' from my side of the family.

Michelle and Anthony were teenagers when I met Paula and they had a tough time as they saw me fallin' head over heels in love. They didn't have a storybook childhood to start with. After I was divorced, Michelle, at seventeen, had to pitch in and help me take care of the house and Anthony when most teenagers were doin' teenager things. She felt, in an understandable way, like she was my and Anthony's keeper. Then along came Paula. Pretty soon, I was practically livin' with Paula over at the Projects while my kids stayed in my house a stone's throw away. We were in touch constantly by phone, and I dropped over my house about a million times a day to make sure all was good. But Paula had still not officially been introduced to my kids.

That was perfect, as far as Michelle was concerned anyway. About this time, Michelle decided she could not like Paula and be loyal to her mother at the same time.

Anthony was a bit younger and found it easier to love Paula. In the beginning, though, even he didn't see Paula as a possible step-mother figure. He may have thought of her as a character. I remember we had this fig tree in my yard, and I told Paula she could get some ripe figs for a fig preserve pie she was bakin'. She'd gone around the fence to my house and climbed a ladder up into the fig tree. Anthony and his little girlfriend Jennifer happened to come home at that moment. "Look," said Jennifer to Anthony, "there's some crazy ol' lady in the fig tree."

It was Paula. Crazy as a fox.

Finally they all officially met; it looked like they kinda liked each other but frankly I didn't think my kids ever dreamed my romance with Paula Deen was gonna go anywhere.

I was wrong. Michelle had sensed it, but hid her fears at first. To her, Paula had always seemed a threat. In retrospect, I guess it seemed that Paula was takin' over her role in the family as well as her daddy. And gosh, it was really tough to figure out who I should be loyal to, my child or my great new girlfriend. *I* knew both of 'em were really nice people, but I also knew that both of 'em were strong willed enough not to budge a bit. So it was really tough. Anthony was another story. He was just kind of a happy-go-lucky kid who probably felt torn between his sister Michelle on one side and Paula and me on the other. He definitely didn't know which side to get on.

There was no way I could fix this thing. I couldn't take sides and that didn't make me too popular with any of them. Michelle was sullen and sarcastic all the time. I guessed she was hurtin' inside somethin' awful. There was a time when Paula had had her fill and felt threatened. She didn't know if she could ever find peace with me, Michelle, and Anthony.

Eventually, I just had to tell Michelle that this was my life she was tampering with. I wasn't going to ignore her feelings, but believe it or not, I told her, I had a stake in my life.

What finally prevailed was that Paula was adult enough not to get on Michelle's level and argue. Eventually Michelle came around and realized what she was doin' was childish. But it would still take some heavy liftin' till things were normal.

I tried to keep control of the situation, but it was pretty loose control. In the end, I had to be the strongest person because I was the only one who knew that what was goin' to happen was what I wanted to happen. It was goin' to be me and Paula and Michelle and Anthony. And Cody. And those stupid little black-and-white dogs. My kids would always have their mother, but now there were more people and pets involved. They just had to learn to deal with it.

I was certain that once they got to know Paula they'd love her. If Michelle could've found something wrong with Paula, it would've made it so much easier for Michelle to keep Paula out of her life, but she couldn't find anything. Not *one* specific thing. Paula's pretty terrific. Michelle's the first to admit that. Now.

Around that time, I even started having some serious trouble with Anthony. It was the academics. He was always actin' out and he thought he was a comedian. He broke up his class at school too many times. I remember he got in trouble and just stayed in trouble, so I had quite a few private meetings with his teachers. In many ways, he was really a tough kid at school. Fact was, he just was not happy at the Benedictine Military High School where my father, my brothers, and I went. It was a family tradition but it wasn't the right place for Anthony. Well, the guidance counselor went to our church and because Anthony is a good kid at heart, the counselor kinda overlooked the fact that my boy had accumulated the fifty demerits he needed to get kicked out of the school. But when Anthony reached seventy-eight demerits, the guidance counselor had his fill and Anthony was finally asked not to return.

I made a decision. "Most dads," I told Anthony, "would throw up their hands and say, 'Now you go to public school, and that's good—it'll save me some money. Benedictine is a private school and all this time it cost me a lot. Now, because of your actin' out, if you get what you need in the public school, fine. If you're still a comedian and you don't get what you need, fine also. It's your life.' "

But then I told him, "I'm not most dads. I've decided you're going to Camden Military Academy, which is a boardin' school, and—my luck—*twice* as expensive as Benedictine. Michelle and I will miss you somethin' awful. But if you make it there, when you come back, you'll be a man. You'll learn that as much as you think you know more than everybody at that school, there's still more you need to learn."

Sendin' him away was the hardest thing I ever did. It was shortly after my divorce and the last thing I wanted my kid to think was that I didn't want him around me and I was taking the easy way out to get him out of my hair by sending him out of town. Frankly, it broke my heart.

Believe me, boarding school was far tougher on me than him. I was a mess. But I did it. I never in my wildest dreams thought I'd send a child of mine out of town and away from me and his life here just for school.

Anthony came home every weekend. Michelle would help me drive him back and forth; that car saw plenty of mileage. Even though our relationship was new, Paula was a doll and also helped me with the driving. Then Anthony discovered the train could also bring him home every weekend and he became a train guy; he got more frequent-flier miles on that train than the engineer.

But without a doubt, sending Anthony to Camden was a great decision. He grew up. I just knew he wouldn't compromise his raising. His character was molded in that military academy. Deep inside, he really knew I was doin' it for him and finally, finally the boy was working as hard as he could to become a man.

So now Paula had met my kids and I'd met hers, but I hadn't yet met her brother, who was her partner in the restaurant business. I'd been hearin' about this Bubba from the first, and the day I finally met him, I immediately liked him. In fact, since I've been married, I've always ended up hanging out with Bubba when Paula's off bein' busy. We enjoy most of the same things: We like to hunt and fish and tell great jokes. I think he approved of me also. If he didn't, I wouldn't be here. Guarantee that: Paula *really* loves that Bubba.

Bubba also had loyalties to Paula's first husband, Jimmy Deen, who took him in and raised him when his parents died. He loved Jimmy Deen. You know, my hat's off to Jimmy Deen. What he did was so admirable, but I didn't want to have to compete for Bubba's friendship. Turned out my brother-in-law-to-be gave his friendship to me pretty durn easy.

I'm sure Bubba thought I was good for his sister, but he's the first to admit he also thought I'd be good for *him*. At the time I met Paula, because she was single, Bubba was havin' to bring her to the airport, fix her tires, change her lightbulbs, mow her lawn, and a whole mess of other guy work—Paula can be high maintenance, you know. Bubba would jokingly hug my neck and say, "When's the weddin'—I *loooooove* you." Honestly, I think he was excited that Paula would finally have some security. He loved her so, he really didn't mind doin' stuff for her, but he wanted somebody to be there full time. Just didn't want it to be him.

Full time with Paula looked good to me and I was gettin' ready to apply for that job. I was starting to feel real serious about this laughin' woman and we'd become best friends. We did everything together.

I think before Paula and I met, she was fightin' for her life at the restaurant. At the Lady & Sons she was, I hate to use the word *mean*, but then she was: Nothin' would get between her and her baby, which was the restaurant, so she was as tough as any employer out there. After she met me, she softened some and so the employees at the restaurant loved me before even Paula did.

The Paula I first met wasn't the Paula she is now. The married guy she was datin' before me did a lotta damage to her self-worth. He was no good.

But I have to thank him for one thing: I learned a valuable lesson about how to answer women's questions. I wasn't as smooth as I am now. Once I almost pushed Paula away from me and ruined my life by runnin' my mouth stupidly.

One night we were in bed and Paula said, "Do you think this relationship's goin' anywhere or should I still date this other guy?" She meant that married man who was still callin' her like crazy since he'd found out she was gettin' pretty serious with someone else.

I thought it was a right weird question, bein' that our relationship definitely was goin' somewhere or I wouldna' been where I was. It seemed to me that she wanted the answer to be "You can date whoever you want to date."

What a dope. Shows you how cool I was with women. Frankly, I thought Paula's question meant she wanted to date more than one person.

My answer was, "I don't give a shit what you do."

Brilliant move for me. Paula was pretty much brokenhearted, but her friends were in town, so she went to the mall with them, crying inside all the time. I couldn't stand it; I'd begun to get the clue I'd given her exactly the wrong response. So, I called her on her cell phone at the mall, told her how I really felt, and she came flying home and into my arms.

Look, I'm a simple guy and I like it when people I love talk simple and true. If she really wanted to date several guys at a time, I would move on. If we were to be together, it was going to be only me. I just didn't get the game she seemed to be playing. I'm not good at games.

Guys, remember this: If something your gal says bothers you, say, "It bothers me." But don't *ever* say, "I don't give a shit what you do."

That don't work.

It ain't the right answer.

You can say, "Yes, I care about you. Yes, this relationship's goin' somewhere. And, yes, get rid of that other asshole."

I also was a little worried about my friends: Would they like Paula?

Well, yeah, I think they did. But she and I stayed so busy, we didn't go to a lotta things featuring my old friends when we first met. My best friend, Buckethead, didn't like her at *all* because I started datin' her and spendin' all my time with her 'stead of him. Buckethead (also known as Frank) and I went to high school together, played football together, and ended up ridin' motorcycles together. We'd go down to Daytona for bike week every March and we would just ride motorcycles together around to the beach. I helped him build his floatin' dock here in Savannah and helped him build a house. Then Paula arrived. He wasn't ready for such interference.

Buckethead is really funny. If you saw his head you wouldn't ask why he has that nickname. Fact is he has a *huge* head. He was an electrician by trade and once somebody told him to go get his hard hat and he said he'd forgotten that hard hat. The other guy said,

"Well, go get a five-gallon bucket and put it on your head. Looks like it'll be a right good fit." After that he was Buckethead.

Buckethead has a catering business. He does low-country boils and chicken, and he has two huge grills. He does a great job catering; I would occasionally help him.

Paula and Buckethead have never really been too friendly and that still applies today. He's since moved up-country a little bit. Sometimes guys don't like when their best friends are carried off by a woman. Buckethead didn't like it at all when I really quit datin' him and married Paula.

Early in our courtship, Paula and I ate out a lot. My kids were still teens and I was bouncin' back and forth from the Projects to my house. Paula worked every day and I worked every day, so we stayed busy without havin' much of a social life.

In the South, we live to eat. I've heard that up north, they eat to live. Here's the only place that you'll wake up for breakfast and wonder what you're havin' for supper. When you go out to supper, you're wondering maybe what tomorrow's supper is gonna be. We had fun, Paula and I, just the two of us. Once, I remember, when I had some crab traps out in the creek, I went and caught a whole bushel of crabs. So I called Paula and I said, "What are we doin' tonight?"

And she says, "I don't know."

I said, "Well, come over and I'll just boil some crabs." So I boiled a bunch of crabs and put 'em on the table, and she came over to the house.

I picked out the best meat from every one of the crabs and fed it to Paula, just drippin' it in her expectant mouth. It was like a Roman orgy. She said she had never felt full offa eatin' blue crabs until I picked 'em all and fed 'em to her.

She liked that I cooked and I ate with such pleasure, just like her. I was beginning to find out from personal experience she wasn't a half bad cook herself. I had to tweak her on a few things and teach her some o' my tricks, but all in all, I came to see that Ms. Paula Deen was good at stirrin' the pots.

One o' the things I think that drew us together and still does is our powerful sense of family. It's not just Paula, it's Paula and her kids, Paula and her brother, Paula and her Aunt Peggy, Paula and her niece, Corrie—with Paula, it's a package. It's a big package, but it's the same feel o' family I have, and I loved that she and I were like two peas in a pod. My children were my heart. Hers, the same. How we understood that in each other!

I have my regrets when it comes to my original family. Nobody knew I was goin' on this train ride, but I sure would have loved to bring my parents along with me to appreciate Paula. Probably the one thing I regret about my youth is losin' my parents when I was too young, before I had a whole lot to give back. I wish so bad that I could have bought them a car or a house or a ticket to Hawaii or somethin' to make their lives easier.

Paula was about the same way with her parents, you know; we were both shortchanged with our parents dying young.

I could have made it so much easier for my momma. When I was small, she'd go to seven different grocery stores to get the best shoppin' deals so we could make ends meet. I never knew what she was doin'. I did go on a few grocery trips with her and I was thinkin', *This is silly; you could buy our food all at one place.* But she would look at meat at one place and vegetables at another place for the best bargains.

And Paula's family was pretty much the same; before she hit the big time, they were definitely coupon clippers. One of the reasons I hit it off so fast with this wild, white-haired gal is that we *got* each other, even without words.

So things were lookin' pretty good. I was fallin' deeper and deeper in love, and I couldn't even believe it myself, I was actually thinkin' about getting married.

One thing I need to get into is this: I gotta tell the truth. I had one bad experience with marriage. It took me a long time to believe things weren't going to go sour with Paula, too. I just knew the relationship was gonna fall apart, even if there were no signs of that. How could it last? I didn't trust the happiness. I must have acted that way, too . . . wary, suspicious.

But every time I saw those blue eyes, I thought, *Maybe, just maybe I'll have another chance at love.*

Paula happened to be on an upswing when we met. She had gone through her terrible times with agoraphobia and poverty and was pullin' out of it. She pulled me along with her to joy. But sometimes I'd fight the joy.

I think we dated three years. Every day I'd wake up and say, "Well, you know, maybe this is the day things will fall apart. Maybe this is the day things'll change. Be strong and expect it, man."

But it never did. My Paula was solid and steady and never changed.

The doubt in me slowly quieted. I realized that Paula might be my true soul mate. Still, I guess I needed to make a real leap of faith in order to commit myself because I wasn't as brave as she was. But the more we were together, the more we wanted to be together.

First Mate's Shrimp Creole

Momma Groover would serve this over a bed of hot white rice along with some creamy coleslaw and corn bread.

PREP TIME: About 1 hour and 10 minutes, including cooking time

SERVES: 4 or 5

¼ cup flour

¼ cup vegetable oil

3 medium-sized onions, chopped

½ cup green bell pepper, chopped small

2 celery ribs, chopped small

2 bay leaves

3 garlic cloves, finely chopped

1 cup tomato paste

3 cups water

1 tablespoon lemon juice

1 cup white wine

2 teaspoons salt

¼ teaspoon cayenne pepper

¼ teaspoon black pepper

One 1-pound box of white rice

2 to 3 pounds cleaned, peeled shrimp

In a large skillet, cook the flour in the oil on a low flame, constantly stirring it until it turns a nice golden brown. Now add your onions, bell pepper, celery, bay leaves, and garlic. Keep stirring, or your roux can stick and burn. Add the tomato paste, mash it around the bottom of the skillet, and cook it for 3 to 5 minutes (it will turn darker). Add 2 cups of water. Stir until the base is nice and smooth—let it simmer for 10 to 15 minutes. Should the base get too thick during the simmerin', just add some of the third cup of water, a little at a time.

Your vegetables should be tender by now. Add any remaining water, the lemon juice, and the wine. Add the salt and cayenne and black pepper, cover the skillet with a tight-fitting lid, and let it cook over low heat for about 30 minutes. Stir everything around once in a while to make sure all is cooking evenly.

Meanwhile, cook the rice according to package directions.

About 20 minutes before you're ready to eat, put the shrimp in the skillet. Stir them around a little and drop your fire to very low so that the Creole just barely simmers and bubbles the least little bit. Y'all want to cook the shrimp good, but take care not to overcook them. Serve over the cooked rice. ⚓

3

I Married Her . . . I Did?

*A Southerner can get away with the most awful kind of insult
just as long as it ends with the words "Bless her (or his) heart,"
as in:*

*If they put his brain on the end of a pin, it'd roll around like
a BB on a six-lane highway, bless his heart.*

or

*He's so bucktoothed he could eat an apple through a picket
fence, bless his heart.*

or

*She can't help bein' ugly, but she could have stayed home,
bless her heart.*

Yes, Paula and I wanted to be together all the time, but I have to admit there was a brief but bad glitch in our relationship. It could have been the end of the Paula and Michael Show before the curtain ever really rose. I guess, though, we learn from everything, and Paula and I managed to walk away, not fatally hurt.

One night we were at the Crowbar, a little bar just down the street. If you go there today, you'll see the same people that have been sittin' at that bar for aeons. Maybe the names have changed, but the characters haven't. It's one of those places. Anyhow, we walk in and two gals are sittin' there. They begin whispering and sayin' dirty stuff, and laughin' in our direction. Paula, bein' Paula, walks over to confront 'em. I didn't realize this at the time, but I think they said somethin' to Paula about me.

I told Paula, "Just leave 'em alone, they're crazy. Nothin' ever happened between us." Paula was pretty jealous. They kept yellin' out stuff and God knows what they told Paula—she never revealed that—but anyway, when we came home, she was angry and aloof. Frankly? Now I was hurt and I really lost my temper.

I said to her, "You know, I need time, I really got to kinda rethink this thing, rethink our relationship. There needs to be trust."

I got all my clothes and moved back home, just a few feet away from where I first met Paula Deen and her poopin' dogs.

It devastated Paula. I felt kinda sick, too, like somebody'd kicked me in the stomach. But you know, I was thinkin' that if Paula was lookin' for somebody without a past, that was not me. I had baggage. And you know my past was maybe even a colorful past, even though it truly did not have anything to do with those girls in the Crowbar. Once I heard someone say that when you get married for the second time, you have to open up your baggage, just like they make you do when you come through customs. You have to show the other person all your stuff. Well, I don't buy that. Maybe it's different for men and women but I felt like I didn't want to have to explain ever' little thing that I did in the past or even the future. There had to be a level of trust.

Havin' life baggage went for her as well as me. I never once asked her about her ex-boyfriend or Jimmy Deen. I really didn't want or need to know anything about that part of her life. I felt like there musta' been an attraction between Paula and those dudes or they wouldna' been together. But most deeply I felt like it was *now*, a brand-new chapter for the two of us. The rest was history.

You just can't keep bringing up your loved one's history and bein' Judge Judy about it, whether your partner acted foolish or not. The past is past.

My movin' back home with my kids didn't last too long; I missed Paula really bad, too. So a couple of days after that, I packed up my clothes again and moved back to the Projects where I belonged, back to my Paula. And we did confront the thing about the jealousy, which is a horrible thing that can break up any relationship. We talked and talked. Paula said my leavin' just about broke her heart. She couldn't go to work. She couldn't be with her friends or sons. She would climb up to the third story of her condo and look out the window to see when I left home for work and when I came back.

Paula and I have been together ever since. I think we both realized that jealousy's a terrible emotion. Forgiveness is much safer. We were committed to each other. We *would* trust each other.

Little did I know that the incident would come up again way after we were married. I thought we'd patched it up. You never know if the patch holds tight. That wound was to open again. Who would have thought jealousy had such holdin' power? It almost sank our boat.

Lesson: Paula forgets nothin'.

One thing we both knew: When I first met Paula, I told her: You know my kids are young. Although yours are a little older, mine are still a work in progress. They're goin' to make plenty of mistakes, and because kids don't come with a set of instructions, we're goin' to have to sit out a lot of difficult times—all of us. So, if we get married, we both have to agree that our kids are very much part of the deal; it's not just the two of us.

It was agreed. There was never a better momma than Paula, and I sure try my hardest to be a good daddy. We could all go on this wild ride together. Funny thing is that none of us knew quite how wild it would turn out to be.

Well, we'd been livin' together two years, and every day I knew more strongly that I wanted to live the rest of my life with this woman.

Paula was safe harbor for me. She was landfall. So, frankly, I decided all by myself that we would get married. I hadn't mentioned it to Paula yet.

Our second Christmas together was coming up, and it meant a lot to both of us to have our families all together. I thought to myself that it would be a perfect time to propose to Paula and make her an honest woman. The ring was the first order of business. I knew Paula was real romantic, but at the same time, the woman liked her jewelry, especially her diamond jewelry, of which she didn't have much then.

One day we read that there was a sale goin' on at Levy Jewelers, so Paula and I drove down to the store just to browse around. At least that's what we told each other. Soon as we arrived, Paula disappeared down to the opposite end of the store and that suited me fine—it would give me more privacy to accomplish my mission. Secretly I was there to buy her a diamond engagement ring, but what I found out later is that she also had a mission. She was plannin' to buy me a magnificent Rolex watch.

So I talked to the guy behind the counter. I was lookin' for a Charles Krypell diamond ring; I'd seen pictures of them in fancy magazines and they were gorgeous. He brought out a beauty. I'm not that experienced a shopper but it seemed like the right thing. We started negotiatin' and I told him what I would give him.

Then I said, "See the gray-haired lady there? If she hears about this conversation, then the deal's off."

Without a doubt, Paula saw me talkin' to the salesperson, but she was still doin' her own shoppin' and hidin' from me, which worked out perfectly, because I knew she wouldn't come over.

The ring was breathtakin'; if you've watched Paula on TV, you've seen it. I'd done my homework on buyin' diamonds and I didn't have to think twice.

"Will you take XX amount?" I asked the jewelry guy. "Go over there, think about it a couple of moments, then come back and tell me yes or no. If it's yes, then we might be able to work a deal."

When he came back, he said yes. I paid for it and walked away with the most gorgeous ring in the history of mankind.

Paula met me at the front of the store and we left together, each hidin' a secret purchase.

Once home, I thought about it. How do I propose? Somehow, I believed it wouldn't have been right just to give her the ring in private. We're not teenagers, we're powerful family people, and it just seemed our families had to be present to bear witness and make it right and proper. Besides, I knew that I had to make a grand presentation: Ms. Paula likes drama, and so do I.

Thinkin' about it, I decided to steal her son Jamie's idea. Jamie had told me some time ago that he'd bought a gift for a girlfriend and wrapped it in ever-diminishing bigger to smaller boxes. Inside each box, he'd put a separate card. The girlfriend had to unwrap each box to get to the prize. I thought it was a pretty neat idea.

So I asked Michelle Nary, my accountant at work, to get some boxes together and draw the cards for me. I'm not so good at this kind of stuff—I don't have the hands for delicate projects. She got me all the boxes. The ring had come inside a small velvet pouch. The outside box was in the form of a gingerbread house. With a card, I put that inside another box and I surrounded the ring box with Paula's favorite candy—Hershey's Kisses, Snickers Bars, stuff like that. Then I put it all inside another box with more candy and another card in it, and inside another box with more candy and another card in it, and then yet another box—so it was kinda like one of those Russian dolls.

Christmas came and all our festive families along with it. We'd each had a fair amount of eggnog and I'd put the package (by now a pretty big package) with Paula's name on it under the tree. We were all gathered in the livin' room. Corrie, Bubba's daughter (who Paula thought of as the daughter she never had), told Paula she ought to unwrap her present first.

At first, Paula refused to be the first to open her gift. She was used to waitin' on the others as she did every year. But her niece Corrie convinced her (and both families were all in on this), so Paula sat down and opened the big box with her name on the outside. Inside was another box and the candy around that box fell out all over the floor. She laughed her fabulous laugh and opened the card. It only had the word **PAULA** written on it. Then she opened the next box and more candy fell out. Paula read the card out loud, which only said **I.** She opened the next box and the card said **LOVE.**

By this time, she's cryin' a little and opens the next box. The card says **YOU.**

She takes a deep breath, goes for the next box, and rips it open. More candy and another card fall out. This card says **WILL**; the next box was torn open and the card said **YOU.**

And my Paula, who can't wait for nothin', gets so excited and yells out, "YES! YES!" even before she gets to the other boxes. My girl's no fool. She guessed what was happening. It took nine boxes in all for the cards to say **PAULA, I LOVE YOU, WILL YOU BE MY WIFE?**

The truth? I thought it would be funnier to write *WILL YOU BE MY GIRLFRIEND? NO—just kiddin'—WIFE.*

Luckily, I'd realized I'd be the only one laughin', so I changed *GIRLFRIEND* to *WIFE* and left out the *just kiddin'* part.

The last box held the gorgeous diamond ring I'd bought almost under her nose. It sparkled like it was on fire. Paula put it on her finger.

Through a bucket of tears, Paula said yes again and again. It may have been the most romantic thing I'd ever done, maybe the most romantic thing any man on the planet had ever done. Paula would never be able to accuse me of being unromantic—I'd just hark her back to the marriage proposal.

So then and there, we set a wedding date. Paula says, "You wanna do it in March or April?"

I said, "It doesn't matter, what do you wanna do?"

She said, "Well, I'm off both times, so whatever you wanna do."

I said, "March." So we decided on March 6, 2004.

Major mistake.

I had forgotten at the time that every year in March, the first week was always Bike Week in Daytona Beach. Me and my best friend at work, Big Bob, and Buckethead and some other guys *never* miss Bike Week.

When the excitement died down, later on at home, I remembered and said to myself, *Oh, my God, I did it, I picked Bike Week for a weddin' day.* But I knew I'd better not change the date because that would not have been a good start to my wedded bliss.

Wouldn't you know it, though, Big Bob took off Bike Week to come to my weddin'. That's friendship in the South.

As I said before I met 'em, I was worried Paula's boys would not be 200 percent on board when they first met me. I worried they might think I was in it for their momma's money. Well, it turned out that they were 500 percent on board and I needn't have worried about that. It only got better with her boys and me: I really do think they love and trust me today as much as I love and trust them. They're my sons, too.

But probably I wouldna been shocked if they also were a little worried at first. It would only be natural. You have to realize that Paula is not just their mother, she is their boss and partner. There's an ol' Southern saying that goes "If Momma ain't happy, ain't nobody happy." It's sure the truth.

Also, the relationship she had prior to me with that real snake of a married man? You can read about that in *her* book, I'm not touchin' it. Her boys fretted terribly about her. I knew Paula had told them that I surely did not need her money, that I was financially secure and had a very good job. What they might not have known is that although we never signed a prenuptial agreement like many thought we should have, both Paula and I protected our kids through our lawyers, setting up special trusts and wills. The one thing we shared was that if anything ever happened to the other, the one that was left would always be guaranteed a place to live. And thank goodness for that because I would not want to give up the gorgeous and spectacular Garaj Mahal in the new house we're building as I write these words.

When we are both gone, everyone will be well taken care of.

So we had no problem figurin' out how our business assets would be shared. We had some wonderful days right before the weddin' and some magic nights.

But there were also some rough times. In the beginnin' my daughter, Michelle, still could not stop diggin' at Paula. The last thing in the world Paula wanted was more feuding with the daughter I loved with all my heart, but Michelle was devastated that she couldn't wrap her daddy around her little finger like she used to. She felt she no longer came first in my life. It wasn't Paula's doin' at all, Michelle says today. Paula was tryin' to love this child, but Michelle would have none of it. She was, as she says today, simply jealous of "the new woman" in my life. A lot of kids feel that way about a step-mother or stepfather. Today I understand that, but at the time it was awful to see. They simply didn't get along, and talkin' to each other was like arguin' with a fence post. Michelle was nineteen and she had a powerful loyalty to me. She felt responsible for me and An-thony, and she looked at Paula as if she was Cinderella's wicked step-mother; she treated Paula worse. She said things that sounded spiteful and mean and Paula tried, she really tried to make things better, but Michelle was fixed in her thinkin'.

One day, Michelle and I had a really strong conversation in Paula's front yard. I asked her to apologize to Paula. I think she did, but I also think she was still havin' none of this weddin' stuff. Today, I've come to believe that Michelle would have liked to pick my bride, but that wasn't in the cards. If the truth be known, she would have liked it best if I'd just go back to her mother, even though she knew that also was never goin' to happen. Paula did not take kindly to that at-titude. Michelle was as cold as a frosted frog to Paula, and Paula, in turn, felt as welcome as an outhouse breeze whenever she entered a room where Michelle was. It was a bad scene.

It created more problems when Paula and I, after lookin' for months for a wonderful place to live, realized that although the house I lived in was kind of shabby, we could never find any more beautiful land and water than the area where the house sat. So we decided to tear down what was there and build a wonderful new home right on my beloved Turner's Creek, where I'd spent so many great childhood hours.

Turns out that Michelle's relationship with Paula got worse when we tore my house down—the house my kids were raised in—to build a bigger, more beautiful house on the same spot for all of us. I think I never realized seeing her childhood home come down was a heartbreak to Michelle, and it was possibly a threat even to Anthony. Even though Paula was gonna make Michelle a beautiful room she could design herself, it didn't matter. Michelle felt she was goin' to be like a visitor in her own house. Anthony, for God's sake, should have been ecstatic. In our old house, he lived on a porch with fourteen windows; it was cold in the wintertime and hot in the summertime. He had bunk beds and a little desk out there. You know, it was horrible. Now he would have anything in the world he wanted in a home that was neither drafty nor hot no matter the season.

Paula confided in me that she finally told Michelle that there was goin' to be a marriage, but if the marriage broke up, it would be Michelle's fault. I think my child must have felt terrible when Paula said that. Michelle never wanted to come between me and my happiness, I know that; what she wanted at that stage was to *be* my happiness. She just couldn't help actin' horrible to Paula.

Around that time, an interesting thing happened. Paula had her wildly popular cookin' show on the Food Network and the producers decided that they wanted to tape our weddin'. So many Americans felt so close to Paula, the Food Network thought they'd love to be invited to the weddin'. In essence we would be getting married in front of millions of people.

So much for a small, intimate affair. Paula loved the idea, mostly because she loved the Food Network and all they'd done for her, but she made a point o' askin' me if I'd mind the tapin' before she gave any answer at all to the producers. Well, initially I wanted our weddin' to be like a small get-together, because it was both of our second marriages. That would be most appropriate. Still, I told her it sounded like fun; I'd never gotten married on TV before. There would even be a bridal shower for Paula before the weddin', also to be taped.

All the weddin' preparations were going along fine but without a doubt, my daughter was gettin' to Paula. Paula was really feelin' hurt now. Not even the sunniest disposition in the world could stand up to naked dislike from your boyfriend's child. It went on for weeks. Michelle and Paula were having words over the dumbest things, like the laundry and whose should be done where.

Finally, it all came to a head. I couldn't believe it when I heard Paula tell a friend that she was considerin' not getting married at all, but that she would go ahead and do it because she had a contract with the Food Network to film the ceremony—but we'd probably go ahead and get a divorce soon after! I could have gone forever without hearing that.

Not gettin' married was not one of my options. I would never have backed out no matter what. I felt that time heals all wounds and that Michelle would come round to lovin' Paula—as she finally did— and vice versa.

At the time, it did not make me feel good at all to watch people hearin' Paula say we were probably going to get divorced soon after the weddin'. I felt that everyone would take it all out of context and think we just got married because she had a television contract; I knew people didn't know the whole story—all they would think was that our marriage was happening because of a damn contract.

Just about killed me.

I wasn't marryin' Paula because anybody wanted me to do it. I was gettin' married because I loved her to death and I wanted to spend the rest of my life with her.

So like with most people, there was friction right up to the day of the wedding. Normal chaos, I like to call it.

I tried to forget Paula ever said any o' those words to other people. Having the wedding filmed was actually turning out to be fun. Everybody loves to have a video of their weddin' to look back on and so did we, not just for us as much as for future generations. I could tell it was going to be neat to have it professionally done by a TV crew.

Also I was a bit nervous. You know, that camera.

I don't take to the cameras like Paula does. Paula's a natural. She knows when to smile, what to say, and when to say it, and even if she ends up sayin' some loopy, crazy thing, her fans love it. But when the camera was on—especially in the early days—I kind of froze. I wouldn't say I'm shy, I just feel I have to be careful I don't say anything that might reflect badly on Paula. Because I watch everything I say, it doesn't come out natural. Whereas Paula, whatever's on her mind comes out of her mouth. I try to edit myself, which is difficult. I end up just bein' quiet, and that doesn't go well on television. So when we first started tapin' the weddin', I was a bit nervous just to be on camera, let alone get married on TV.

My future bride's boys helped me out. They saved the day! Paula had a wedding shower at the Projects that the Food Network also filmed, and without tellin' a soul, Jamie and Bobby dressed up as bridesmaids. Their long dresses were fluffy and feminine and fabulous. Bobby ran around singin', "I feel pretty, oh so pretty . . ." It was not until they put on these bright-colored bridesmaids' dresses that I had the big laugh that allowed me to relax.

I said to myself, *Now, I should not have a problem puttin' on a tuxedo and bein' myself on television if those kids can let themselves be filmed as giggly bridesmaids.* It kinda broke the ice. But I can guarantee you won't ever see 'em in bridesmaid dresses soon again.

Things were still pretty dicey between Paula and Michelle. One day, Michelle informed me that under no circumstances would she be in the wedding party. I told her, "Well, that really disappoints me but this is your life. You have this one opportunity to make things better with Paula, so make your decision but know one thing: You're goin' to have to live with the consequences forever."

Well, she was pretty adamant about not bein' part of any weddin'. The last date came up where she'd be able to get her bridesmaid's dress and I called her up and said, "Last chance. If you're prepared to live with bad feelings the rest of all our lives, go ahead and don't be part of the biggest day in my life."

Well, right then and there she changed her mind. I hadn't been so happy in a coon's age! I told her that Paula and I wanted so much for her to be there and she was so doin' the right thing by changin' her mind.

But a real good relationship sure didn't happen overnight. Michelle's change of heart about the wedding wasn't the end of the bad feelings between Michelle and her stepmother-to-be.

I was feelin' better about allowing our wedding day to be taped because we'd decided only to tape the reception for the show. We'd still be keeping the most important part of our weddin' private because the ceremony itself would be in a small chapel, which only held about a hundred people, just enough for family and some friends. Big Bob, a colleague and great friend from work, came with his dear wife Jan. The only other friend I invited to the wedding was Buckethead and he did not come.

Afterward, we would hold a reception where the Food Network's cameras would be invited. It seemed like there were about four thousand people at that reception. Well, maybe not four thousand—maybe five hundred. The reception was held at Paula's restaurant, The Lady & Sons, and she'd arranged to serve my favorite cake, banana nut with cream cheese icing, which my momma used to make for me. So, in a way, my momma was there too.

It turned out to be a beautiful reception, but I did tell Paula, "My next wedding, I will *not* hold my reception at The Lady & Sons."

She said, "Well, you can take that to the bank, big boy."

That's what I love best about Paula. We are *always* laughin'.

The weddin' ceremony took place in the Whitfield Chapel at Bethesda School for Boys, which is the oldest functioning orphanage in the country; it turned out to be everything anyone could have wanted. My brother Hank, the priest, officiated and my blood pressure was so high, my ears were hot. And I don't have a blood pressure problem. Whitfield is probably the most intimate wedding chapel ever built. Brandon Branch, Paula's brilliant, can't-live-without-him assistant, decorated it. He's just . . . remarkable. Just to see all the family there—I think I was overcome. Let me say this: I don't cry a lot. Don't know if I ever had many tears, or I lost all my tears, or my tears dried up, or what happened to those tears, but I felt like bawlin' like a baby. The emotion was there. I never felt like that in all my life.

I cried. Shhhhhhh. I don't think anyone saw me.

Paula was a dream walking, absolutely magnificent. This beauty with the sea blue eyes was marrying me. Imagine: a gorgeous, lovable woman who could make you laugh. Without doubt my cup ran over. My soul mate had arrived and I was smart enough to recognize her, even with the poopin' dogs.

We'd rented a horse and buggy to take us to the church: It made me feel like royalty. After the reception, the same horse and buggy took us to the little bed-and-breakfast called the Planters Inn, where we were to stay for our first night as man and wife.

Funny, we were so busy talking to everyone and getting married and all, we'd hardly had anything to eat at our own reception, and so, in the middle of our weddin' night, we got up and walked out the door to Tim's Burger, where we had us a feast. Funny what you remember: It was around three in the mornin' and we were feelin' terrific, and there was a bunch of kids from a local design school havin' burgers too. Maybe they were just feelin' their oats or maybe they had a little buzz on, because one of 'em said, as cocky and rude as you please, "Gosh, what are y'all old folks doin' out so late?"

I told him, "Go ahead and eat your food, buddy, while you still have your teeth, and just pray that you can get up and go like we do when you're our age. But come to think of it, the way you're talkin' to us, there's a good chance you may not make it to our age."

We left the next day for The Cloister on St. Simons Island in Georgia, an absolutely beautiful resort; you feel like you're in another country. Later on, Gordon Elliott, Paula's wonderful producer, gave us a trip to Alaska for a couple of weeks, and that was great fun.

But with all the happiness and glory, I want to tell the truth: There sure were some mixed emotions at the wedding chapel that day. Amidst all the beauty, maybe just because I'm human, I felt a little uneasy and that feeling would take a while to whip down. As I write this book, just after our fifth anniversary, I can say with all my heart that Paula and I were made for each other, that we are righter than right. But the day I got married, married for the second and last time, I had some sadness.

First of all, a long time ago I'd made a vow that I would do this marrying thing once and never do it again. And here I was, doin' it again. Plus, I still had in the back o' my mind that Paula might be marrying me only 'cause she was forced to, for business. And so I was nervous because I felt like my future was in question. Instead of it bein' the happiest moment, I was wonderin' where our relationship was going to go after the wedding day.

If I had known then what I know now—that our relationship was going to fulfill every dream we both had—I could have done away with the queasies on our weddin' day. If I had known then what I know now: that Paula was feelin' at her wit's end when it came to her relationship with Michelle, and that's why she figured she might be forced to get a divorce. How could she live with a man whose child hated her? If I had known then what I know now—that my daughter and my new wife would grow to be lovin' and supportive friends—I would have been happy as a clam at high tide.

Now? I'm the luckiest man alive, and I know my wife feels the same way. The world loves Paula Deen to death, but she's mine to go home with. And I'll say this: She is never, never, never, never, never, never boring.

You know there's something to be said about marryin' someone who comes up in the same place you did. Probably both of us could have successfully married Northerners or Westerners or Easterners (well, maybe not), but because I'm a man of the Deep South I just love that I've married a woman of the Deep South. We understand each other even before the other speaks.

There's a pride in belonging to this special place and there is a powerful sense of carrying on the heritage when you marry someone from here. I never really understood that when I was young, and I probably would have never known it so well unless I traveled. There's just a diff'rent feel down South. You're taught very young to say "Yes, sir" and "No, sir" and "Yes, ma'am" and "No, ma'am." You're taught to have manners, to say "Thank you" and "No, thank you," and to stand up when a woman comes to the table. You're taught that as a little bitty child.

Aside from the politeness of people, there's something about the smell of the land and the water here that's different from any other place in the world. I shared this pride with my new wife even on our weddin' day, even when I was feeling a little nervous.

The scent of the azaleas, the hanging moss, even the muddy marsh at low tide: It all smells good to me. The lizards creepin', the creeks flowin', the colors of the fish jumpin'—you never did see such colors anywhere else.

There have always been stereotypes about Southerners that are horrible and I'm sure that casting directors search high and low to find some o' these stereotypical dumb-ass characters to put on TV and make 'em really look like they are the core of the South. I hated the movie *Deliverance*. I hated the cracker types, the brutal and ugly weirdos that some people have come to associate with this part of the land because of damn garbage movies like that. Too many people think that because some of us talk slow, we think slow. It's so not so. My Paula, the typical Southern woman, has one of the quickest brains on the planet. Sure, there are bad apples everywhere you grow up, and we've had some unfortunate history here at home, especially about civil rights, but the South has managed to grow up and grow wiser 'bout that. The South for me is homeland, home sweet home, and although we go to some spectacular places, until we hit that road to Savannah, U.S.A., Paula and I never really feel at home.

You know what? The face of the South for me, the most blessed, the most colorful, the most extraordinary spirit of the South for me, is Georgia's daughter, Paula Deen. And I married her. I did? Yes, I did.

Sailor's Sausage-Stuffed Pork

This is a delicious and easy recipe. Your crew will love ya!

PREP TIME: About 1 hour, including cooking time

SERVES: 4

1 fresh pork tenderloin, about 12 inches long

1 smoked pork sausage, about the same size as the loin. You can cut the sausage if it's too long so it will fit inside the loin.

¼ cup white wine

Worcestershire sauce

Salt

Black pepper

Garlic powder

Paprika

FIG SAUCE

1 tablespoon butter

3 tablespoons apricot jam

1 pint fresh figs, cleaned and halved

Preheat the oven to 350°F.

Wash and wipe dry the pork tenderloin. Run a long, narrow-bladed knife down the center of the tenderloin lengthwise, making a tunnel in the loin.

Now pierce the smoked sausage with a fork in several places. Beginning at the large end of the tenderloin, run the sausage down the center of the pork. Cut off any sausage that's longer than the tenderloin. Rub down the tenderloin with the white wine.

Place the tenderloin in a roasting pan. Sprinkle the outside of the pork with a little Worcestershire sauce. Season with salt, pepper, garlic powder, and paprika. Roast for 35 to 45 minutes, or until the internal temperature of the pork is 160°F.

While the pork is in the oven, melt the butter in a saucepan over a medium flame. Add the jam and when it's melted, add the fresh figs. Stir at a simmer for a couple of minutes. Set aside and keep warm.

Take the pork out of the oven and let it rest for 5 to 10 minutes. Slice, and serve with the sauce. ⚓

4

Fame Swamps Me

Back in the nineties a woman named Lorena Bobbitt became really famous for an act that terrorizes us guys when we even think about it. She got mad at her husband and cut off his penis.

A whole lot o' jokes, limericks, and T-shirt slogans built up after the incident. This is my favorite.

A husband and wife were driving on the highway and arguing, and she accused him of infidelity. She got so mad during the argument that she pulled a Lorena Bobbitt and then threw her husband's penis out the car window. Driving behind them was a small girl and her daddy, and sure enough, that penis came flying and landed splat on their car's windshield.

"What's that, Daddy?" asked the little girl, alarmed.

"Just a bug," answered her father, who didn't want to frighten her.

"Well," said the little girl, "that bug sure had a big dick."

I've often wondered about the nature of fame—who gets to be famous? I can only speak from personal experience. Who gets to be famous apparently is a talented, slightly bawdy but delicious, butter-lovin' cook whose laugh can make the crankiest of the cranky smile.

But who also gets to be famous, again in my own experience, is anyone who is publicly *attached* to the ones the world admires and loves—or despises and hates, as the case may be. In other words, fame has kind of a Velcro character; it even sticks onto people who just hang out with the truly famous—like me.

I think a man is not only the person he was born to be but also the person he was meant to be. I was born to be a man of the sea, a man of boats and fishin' and island explorin', and it looked like that was pretty much all I would ever be, and that was okay with me. It would be just the finest life if that's all it was. But then there was Paula. And my life took on other levels completely—and one of those levels was fame. Without a single doubt, I would have felt complete if I'd only had the first part of my life, the part I was born to. When I take the helm of a ship, I am so thrilled I can't believe people pay me to do it. But then, to have climbed aboard the Paula ride—well, God apparently had other plans for me. How fine it is to be recognized by nice people, to meet so many strangers and make them friends. The kind of celebrity status I seem to have fallen into is exciting and fun, and I never did lose the person I was. I have both lives, one involving a level of fame I never saw, let alone imagined would be mine.

My wife and I live in each other's story instead of just listening to the other talk about what happened that day. In a strange way, what happens to Paula happens to me. We work together, we play together, we travel together, we eat together, we sleep together; she's part of me and I am part of her. Paula has begun to know well the life I was born to. She's come out on shift jobs with me when I was dockin' these majestic ships and she just loves it. We go out on our small boats and our Jet Skis, and Paula has come to love the feel of the wind in her hair and the spray in her face as I do. I must admit, I rarely cede control of any boat to her; I'm not so good at bein' a passenger on a boat. But she's okay with that.

In return, I apparently got to be kinda famous. I share in her life's story every day. I am invited to every business meeting she has. I'm welcome on every trip she takes, every show she films. I watch her as she charms America and often, I'm invited on the shows along with her. Fame comes along with having your face on *Good Morning America*, I've discovered.

So, how does fame express itself? Well, usually, in the nicest of ways—in pleasant, flattering, excitin', funny attentions from others.

Sometimes, though rarely, fame comes in pretty aggravatin' forms. Fame can swamp a person if he's not careful.

Here's the fun part. Do you know that in Savannah, Georgia, there's an always-sold-out bus tour devoted just to Paula Deen? In 2009 it cost fifty-six dollars to take a four-hour tour that drives people to see her restaurants, where she buys her vegetables, where she first lived when she came to this town, where she buys flowers and furniture, where my tugboat is docked, where her favorite Savannah view is, and lots more places dear mostly only to Paula Deen. Who goes on this bus tour? People from Savannah come on the tour, you might be surprised to hear, but also people from New York City, Detroit, San Francisco, Ho-Ho-Kus, Wichita—you name the place, they're on that bus. I asked a friend of ours who took the tour to try to find out just why guests are willin' to sit on a bus so long just to be near things and people in Paula's life. He asked a woman, "What's the deal with Paula? Why do you think her popularity merits a whole bus tour? Where are you from and why are you on this tour?"

"I'm from Lewisburg, Pennsylvania," the woman answered with a grin, "and why I'm here is simple. I love Paula Deen. I love her because she looks like me, she sounds like me, she's roundish and funny and every day, she eats like me: If a little food drops out of her mouth while she's cookin' on television, she don't care. She makes me laugh. She *is* me. She may not know it, but she's my friend. I really, honestly feel that."

That doesn't surprise me. She's my friend, too, for many of those same reasons.

The bus tour usually ends up with a lunch at Uncle Bubba's Seafood and Oyster House—the restaurant Paula owns with her baby brother, the incomparable Uncle Bubba. Make no mistake: While the guests are gobbling down their fabulous crab cakes, they're keeping a sharp eye out for a possible appearance of The Lady, and maybe even me. Can you believe that?

You better not get too high and mighty when you're swept along in this fame thing by someone else's glamour, I found out. Once I was workin' the tables at Uncle Bubba's, just walkin' around talkin' to people, and, as I usually do, I asked one group at the table, "How y'all doin'? Where y'all from? What y'all eatin'?"

One little old lady looked up at me, wrinkled up her eyes, and said, "Who *are* you?"

Fame's fleetin'.

Uncle Bubba's has the finest seafood in all Savannah. It's a bigger restaurant than The Lady & Sons and can accommodate the crowds better, so that's why the bus tour ends up for lunch there. I particularly like the shirts worn by the waitresses at Uncle Bubba's. One says IF YOU AIN'T GETTIN' IT AT HOME, YOU CAN GET IT AT UNCLE BUBBA'S. Another says REAL MEN SHUCK WITH BOTH HANDS. Yet another proclaims I CAME FOR UNCLE BUBBA'S OYSTERS AND I LEFT WITH CRABS. You get the idea. It ain't a real formal place.

People come to Savannah, Georgia, to see the famed squares and plazas, the hanging moss, and the marvelous waterfront, but a destination stop is always that fountain of Southern dining, the restaurant Paula owns with her boys, The Lady & Sons. The fans who wait in a line that stretches almost to South Carolina are so kind and so eager for a touch of her. Maybe sometimes a little *too* eager for my taste. When I'm at the restaurant, waves of fans come over to talk and ask me to sign somethin'. It's so much fun but kind of weird actually that so many people think I'm a celebrity when I'm just a tugboat captain. I have gotten to know quite a lot of strangers and call them friends, but without a doubt, any fame I have is because Paula is so successful and I married Paula. Paula earned her success slowly. I became famous overnight because I had the good luck to marry her. Paula had time to adjust a little bit, but in the beginning, I thought it was extremely strange that people were takin' my picture and comin' up for a touch of me. All I am is a regular guy who's pretty handy on a boat.

Listen—people surround me but who they really want to see is Paula. If they can't see Paula, then if they could see her sons, Jamie or Bobby, or me, or her Aunt Peggy, or Bubba or Bubba's son, Jay, or Jellyroll or Dora, who work in the restaurant, or anybody that has anything to do with Paula, that's second best. They wanna see the family because they wanna talk to somebody who knows what Paula's *really* like.

News flash: They already know what Paula's really like, even if they only watched her once on television. What you see is what you get, what I got—that's the real Paula.

Bubba told me that he remembered a cruise our whole family once took together: A gentleman walked over to him and Paula and said, "Y'all remind me of the damn Mafia. Y'all stick together so close." Bubba took that as a compliment.

• • •

If we're talkin' about fame, let me set a scene for you. Last night Paula was away and I just had a yearnin' for her fried chicken, so I drove over to The Lady & Sons real early, like around five o'clock, before dinner hour.

Didn't matter. Early, late, there's always a line around the block. I parked, pulled my hat down over my face, and quietly tried to enter a side door, but no matter. The crowd on line seemed to get happy and excited when they spotted me. In a moment I was surrounded by the most loving, grateful, and faithful fans who begged for my autograph, a kiss, a word—*anything* from Paula's husband.

"It's only me," I want to say, "out for some fried chicken just like you. I'm not Paula, I'm not famous, I ain't no star," but it doesn't matter. Guess it's my white beard they recognize and those faithful line huggers pull at my jacket, stroke my arms, and thrust out their books for my signature. Me: Michael Groover, Southern boy, tugboat guy.

Then the questions start comin':

Where's Paula?

What will the two of you do for Christmas?

Will you be on her show again this week?

Michael, can you give me a kiss?

Michael, are you ever in Philadelphia?

Do you still run a tugboat?

Michael, do you have a brother?

Michael, do you ever get a chance to cook?

Michael, what's Paula really like?

Do you ever have fights?

Is it hard being married to the most famous woman on the planet?

Michael, I can cook too!

I don't want to lie; part of me loves it to death. Damn, fame is fun.

I seem to have a following; people write to me and send me stuff, just as they do Paula, although how the hell that really happened I'm still not positive. Fans feel they know me—*really* know me—from sightings on Paula's shows, in her books, at her readings, and other personal appearances I make. It's terribly flattering and I'll never *not* be surprised at it. I didn't earn it but it's great fun and I happily accept those wonderful fans!

Here's the part that's not so much fun about fame. If truth be told, I'll always feel kinda like Tom Arnold, Roseanne Barr's ex-husband. He became famous because of Roseanne. He ended up with his own television show after they were divorced, so I guess he had his own showbiz talents and he transcended the celebrity that came from his ex-wife. Since I plan to be married to my wife for, like, forever, I guess I'll never know if people come up for my autograph because I'm me or because I'm Paula's husband. And you know what? At this point, I don't care. I just have such a good time being both Michael Groover *and* Paula Deen's husband.

In other ways, fame can be pretty aggravatin'. Fame can swamp a person if he's not careful. There is another downbeat side of any kind of fame and even though it's minimal, you just have to deal with it. Once Paula and I were havin' an intimate conversation at a restaurant in town, and a woman came up and said, "I don't wanna interrupt you, but I'd like to tell you about my grandmother's diabetes."

Just like that. Well, that's part of the fame deal. These people've come a long way, they wanna talk about their grandmother to Paula, they wanna tell her a story—everybody has a story. I think I take it in stride and she sure does. I mean, you'll never find anyone who'll be more genuinely interested in your grandmomma's diabetes than Paula Deen; she's just like that. I've gotten pretty good at bookmarkin' where I left off and then pickin' up my conversations when the people leave. You can't be rude.

If you crave privacy, if you want your anonymity, don't be famous. Part of your life always belongs to other people.

Another downside is that sometimes you don't know who your real friends are. I'm sure I'm invited to more functions and to be a member of more country clubs than I woulda ever been offered before I married Paula.

People often say to me that I'm just the same, even though the money part of fame can easily be a life changer. We all know the stories of people who got into drugs or too much booze or lost all their money. It can also create animosity between husband and wife; I'm sure that happens to some people and I'm sure prayin' it doesn't happen to us. Fame's kind of unpredictable—with many well-known people, you can't figure out what others see in them. I guess I know why Paula's so beloved by fans. You know, she's just got an infectious personality. She is brutally honest. In today's times, to find somebody on TV who's honest and sincere is a rarity. A whole mess of hometown people knew her when she was just selling sandwiches, and now that she's somewhat beyond sandwiches, she still feels and acts as though that's all she does.

Funny, Paula really had a sense of the future before it ever happened. She asked me, probably 'bout four years ago, "I feel somethin's comin' on, Michael. What do you think it is? Why do people treat me as nice as they do?"

"Probably 'cause you're real," I told her. "Ain't nothin' phony about you, girl. People want to see real, they're tired of fake. You go to Hollywood, and everything out there's kinda fake."

She just smiled, happy as a clam in high tide when I said that. Actually, I predicted when she started datin' me that her career would skyrocket when we were a serious couple. I told her that as a joke, but it came true so I'm sticking to my story—I made her what she is!

Fame takes us to wild places with wild and unexpected things happenin', but no matter how wild, you can bet that somehow Paula handles it. If I, for example, were ever on a stage in front of millions of people with a television camera trained on me and, say, my britches fell down to my knees—I'd want to crawl into a hole. I'd slink back to my boat and never want to hear the word *fame* again.

But that just recently happened to my Paula. Can you believe it?

We were at the South Beach Wine and Food Festival in Florida, and Paula's prancing up and down the stage bein' Paula, when all of a sudden she felt somethin' funny happening. Seems her pants were loose on her to begin with and the producers had hooked two weighty microphone packs on the back of her waistband. She was also wearing Spanx, which made her butt slippery, she says. In the middle of talking to the audience, her pants fell completely down to her knees. There she was, full butt exposed, or moon over Miami, as she later put it. Well, for most people, that could be the end of their career. Paula pretty much laughed it off and didn't miss a beat. She grabbed up her pants, strutted up and down the stage still clutchin' 'em, and asked the gasping audience, "Did y'all see anything?"

And they all yelled back, "Yes!" I was in the audience that mornin' and I about died of embarrassment for her when I saw it happen. I also know everything can't go perfectly, and if anybody could pull it off, Paula could pull it off. (Sorry. Couldn't help myself.) So I didn't get too excited. That's one of the funny moments fame brings. Stuff like that happens to her all the time and most people woulda stressed out about it for years and probably had to go to their therapist. But she about died laughin' and she was on *The Oprah Show* the next day, still laughin' about it.

Another time, Bobby, Jamie and his wife, Brooke, Bubba, and I were sitting in the front row at *The Oprah Show* and Bobby had a brand-new suit on. Paula and Oprah were bakin' a cake and all the ingredients were in these little glass ramekins. Well, Paula began to pour in the vanilla and wouldn't you know it, she dropped the whole glass ramekin into the mixer bowl as the blades were swirling around.

It was mayhem. Batter exploded, flying everywhere, backward, frontward, sideways. Paula and Oprah took off runnin'. Bobby, in the front row, ducked to avoid the batter, which he definitely did not want on his new suit. His expression as those clumps of batter headed toward the audience and him was priceless, and the camera caught it.

YouTube showed the segment about a million times.

Oprah said it was her favorite cooking segment on her show ever.

There's a solid reason I'm able to stay grounded, stay myself even in the face of so much looniness, money, and attention, and I'm grateful for it. Frankly, if I was out o' work or had a menial job, I'd be in trouble; I might have felt some jealousy of all that love and all those laughs comin' my wife's way. But I feel like I can live in a bubble of fame and still be the man I was born to be for a good reason. I am successful and I make good money on my own path to success. It can't hold a candle to Paula's fame or fortune, but that doesn't matter. If I didn't have my own work and identity, I think fame could have corrupted our relationship, as it has done to so many others we know.

My work's great, but its demands are also the one problem I have.

This job I love requires me to be there. My wife also needs me to be with her; her career demands that she travel frequently. We both work hard to find a balance.

I'd love bein' with Paula, and I would love bein' with her even if she wasn't famous, but it's neat that everywhere we go, people know us. Really, I strongly feel that all we have in life is family, so how great is it that wherever Paula and I go, people treat us like family. You know, if you saw another celebrity, say Beyoncé, you'd think, *Oh, she sings great. She's wonderful. I wish I had the nerve to ask her for an auto-graph.* But you probably wouldn't ask her to come eat at your house. You probably wouldn't even think about approaching her.

But people ask us all the time, "Please come to eat." They wanna cook for Paula and they want her to cook with them and be part of their families. So I don't care if we go to Chicago or White Plains, a big city or a small town, people know her and love her and people wanna talk to her. It's a neat feelin'. Fame? Fame is the magic of Paula. Fame is when we go to North Dakota and we honestly feel like we got family there; that's how nice and respectful of us the people are. Everybody knows Paula, even in Nome, Alaska. The downside of course is that you really can't take people up on it. We're so busy, we've got so many commitments that we can't go home with people and kick off our shoes and eat with them. But it is still mega-flattering that people want you to be part of their families.

I'm like any other fan, fame gets to me too, and I got a huge kick outta talkin' to Jay Leno, 'cause he likes cars and I like cars. Paula's treasured assistants, Brandon Branch and Theresa Feuger, love Oprah and they sure got a kick out of meeting her and her best friend, Gayle, backstage at *The Oprah Show.*

You know what? In my heart of hearts I know that I'm probably the reason Paula's meetin' and greetin' all these stars. Without me, it'd never happen. I'm kiddin'—I'm kiddin'.

Sometimes fame gets us caught in the middle of stuff that ain't none of our business. For instance, Paula's the spokesperson for Smithfield ham. One year, there were big union protests because the plant in Tar Heel, North Carolina, was nonunion and the union wanted to unionize it. What did she know about all that? Nothin'. But Paula was unjustly targeted by the press just because she was the spokesperson for a product she had loved since childhood. There she was, stuck in the middle of union negotiation, a business in which she had no expertise. All of a sudden, everywhere we went, people were askin' my wife if she approved of Smithfield ham not having unions in all their shops.

She was even startled by someone she loves, the fairest of all television interviewers, Larry King on *Larry King Live,* who asked her, "Would you meet with the union people?" Now, all the Smithfield ham products Paula endorses are made in a union plant, so she said yes, of course! She felt like she was correct in sayin' she'd meet with the union.

Whoa! The trouble was that Paula has big trouble sayin' no. Her people (all famous people have their own people, as in "My people will call your people") were pretty upset about it. It even made me a little wary and nervous. You had a lot of angry people walking around with angry signs. I didn't think any of the protesters were violent, although you don't know that. You don't know, you can't predict what some people are gonna do. I mean, *the pope* got shot. It could be one in a million people, but there could be a crazy out there.

That's when we decided that it wouldn't be a bad idea if Paula had a bodyguard. So, now she has one, Hollis Johnson. Hollis is much more than a bodyguard, he's a friend and loyal companion and one o' my favorite people. He calls himself Paula's son even though their complexions sure don't match. She calls him the "black sheep" of the family. Hollis watches her very, *very* carefully when we're out on the road. He watches that she doesn't trip when walkin' down a flight of stairs and he watches that some overeager fan doesn't get too close.

In case you haven't guessed, I'm just crazy about Paula. First of all, I am so proud of her as a businesswoman. People don't realize how instinctively brilliant she is: I mean, of course she's into food, but if she'd set her mind on brain surgery, she'd'a been the finest brain fixer in the country. She just never gives up till she gets the gold ring on the merry-go-round. But asking her to negotiate a union dispute is maybe asking a little too much, don't you think? I'll tell y'all, she has so much on her plate but she's able to juggle fifty balls at once; I don't know one person who can do what she does.

For me, the best part of Paula is that there's no one like her for cuddlin' in our big ol' bed, she's funny as all get-out, she cooks pretty good, and she's gorgeous. What I didn't really count on when we married was the fallout that comes along with the fame she generates. It's pretty invigoratin'. A couple of decades ago this gal was almost on welfare, stuck in her home with agoraphobia, and nobody knew or recognized her except her kids and the bill collectors. Now the whole world wants a piece of Paula, and by extension, sometimes they seem to want me. It's good for the ego.

Mostly it's grand fun but I got to tell you sometimes when strange stuff happens because of her celebrity it leaves me at a loss for words—and actions. Sometimes I feel like a perfect storm wave has just swamped me and it takes all I got to come up for breath and—this is the hard part—act gracious. I ain't no Brad Pitt and I'm not so quick with the right thing to say.

Let me give you an example. You know, it's kinda difficult, not only because of the people and the conversations; I really like to talk to people, so that isn't a problem. It's not really a stretch for me to talk to people about Paula's upcoming events or how proud I am of her accomplishments. But when it gets a little wild I get stuck.

I was in the Chicago airport bathroom one time, standin' at a urinal doin' my business, and damned if the guy next to me don't ask me if I was Michael. Guy was urinating and striking up a conversation at the same time. So I mutter, "Gosh, yes, I am."

And the guy sticks out his hand to shake mine.

Pardon me? That far I couldn't go.

"'Scuse me for not shakin' hands," I told him. "But I know you haven't washed yours and since I'm not finished, I sure haven't washed mine." He looked at me like I was some sort of cleanliness nut and mumbled something about how sure he understood, but I think he was a little insulted.

Then sometimes you don't want to be recognized. Occasionally Paula will put on a baseball cap. She doesn't have her hair done and is wearing no makeup, and there she goes, just cruising through the airport at five o'clock in the morning and no one blinks an eye. But people still recognize me; I don't blend in real well because they always see the Santa Claus in my face. The more literary types always think I'm Ernest Hemingway come back to life.

Paula can pass for a tourist when she wants to but once she opens her mouth to talk or laugh, it's all over. Dead giveaway. One time we were in Vegas and Paula was wearin' a wig. We were eatin' at a restaurant and naturally people recognized me, and they looked at me pretty funny because here was Paula Deen's husband bein' kissed and *handled* by some brunette. Lord, the whispering! When Paula opened her mouth to talk, you could almost hear them saying to each other with relief, "Well, that's no brunette, that's Paula Deen." So they would come over and say, "Are you Paula?" And then she says, "Yeah, and I got a wig on!" Riiiiight. Like they hadn't figured that out. Actually, we had the best time with that wig. I've got the pictures.

General friendliness can sometimes be misinterpreted. I've learned to watch myself in that instance. There are some people you meet, you know they wanna go the limit, past bein' friendly and all. One time I met these three sisters. And one asked had I ever been with three sisters?

I said, "Well, I'm with y'all now."

The other sister said, "No, we mean have you ever really *been* with three sisters?"

I said, "I'm with y'all now."

She said, "You know what I mean."

And I said, "Well, I hope you know what I mean."

It can be wild. I mean, you have to be on your toes. And you know, you gotta watch your hand placements. I've had two different women ask me if I'd sign one of their boobs. And my crazy wife Paula, says, "Oh, go ahead, Michael." And I have hold of the pen like I'm operating, and what could I do but sign? I mean, I'm kiddin' around; I'm friendly but not *that* friendly. Huggin's a big part of the South and I'll hug all right, but like I say, you got to watch those hand placements.

Hey—I'm not complainin'. Most of it's so much fun; I never realized my life could hold such laughs as those I get with Miz Paula. But sometimes fame has a way of taking over, of really swamping the boat. We were goin' to Arizona and people stopped us cold at the airport because they wanted pictures of us. Paula's constitutionally unable to say no, she cannot let a fan down, and she was beggin' me to stop and pose for photos. But I knew we had to get through security and get on the plane in twenty minutes. She remembers her hard history—how difficult it was to get along, even to get out of her house for years and years, and now, here are these strangers pushin' love at her. Now I've learned that's not a real big drawback. You miss a plane, another one comes. In fact it's kinda refreshing and exhilarating to have people come up to you and speak to you with such warmth and admiration in their faces.

When the focus is only on me, I've learned how to deal. Like if I go into my regular grocery store to pick up a few items, at first people would stop me to ask about Jamie and Bobby and their new book, or about Paula's memoir, or about what she's doin' now and how can they get a table in the restaurant, and just when I finish answering those questions, there's another group of people wanting to know anything and everything about Paula and her family. I'd pretty much be stuck in one spot, never being able to move even to snag a pound of sweet butter from the shelf. Now I've learned how to do my shoppin'. I just tell people to walk along with me as I shop—and they do. They follow me from one end of the store to the other as I take care of my shoppin'. When we get to the checkout counter, they don't have any groceries and I'm finished, so I don't mind talkin' but I do have to multitask.

I also have to remember that as much fun as bein' famous can be, you gotta be careful. If your next-door neighbor does something stupid, it's just stupid. If Paula or I do something stupid, shit, it's the mornin' news: It's time to get the pen and paper out for tomorrow's gossip column.

I gotta say what my particular gripe about fame is: the Internet. Most people are just so kind and funny and good-natured but sometimes it about kills me personally to see some of the unfair and untruthful things that have been said about her on the Web. When you're famous, you're fair game, I guess. Lucky Paula doesn't even know how to get on the Internet, but I do.

I think posting on Web sites and blogs is the most unfair way of voicing a strong negative opinion because you can be anonymous there. You don't have to own up to anything and sign your name like in a newspaper editorial. You don't have to be accountable for your words. You can say nasty, filthy things about people. You can lie. You can say your grandaddy loved Paula so he followed her cravin's and because he ate too much butter, one day he up and found himself with high cholesterol and it was Paula's fault. So just because my wife's a rock star who craves butter above all things, that makes her a cholesterol raiser, say some loony birds. You have no way of responding or countering or talking to these people.

Ahhhh, I think, *if everyone thought and did like me, it would be a perfect world, I being a perfect person.*

At one time, Paula would read those things. It would break her heart.

"There's some people there who would never be happy or pleased with anything. So concentrate on the ones who you can make happy," I always advise.

But my wife doesn't listen. She could read ten thousand comments that praised her and two that were bad, and the bad ones would make her so sad, you wouldn't believe it. She would wanna make those two people know her better or she would want to know *how* could two people say stuff like that about her?

I told her that she can't please everyone, certainly not those mean-spirited people. Until some angry-at-Paula person signs her name, until that person allows her opinions to be rebutted or even answered, I feel those writers are cowards. Say what you think, but sign your name. Anonymous Internet comments definitely have a downside because every star out there—I don't care who it is—has a group on the Internet that hates her or him, a group that talks mean and untrue. Few stars take it so personally as my Paula. I mean, deep inside, she knows that most Internet criticism don't mean beans. She knows that she's allowed to misbehave sometimes and if her fans take offense, that's okay too. Even if she was a well-behaved person all the time, some would read bad stuff into things she said or did no matter how innocently. That's fame's ugly underbelly for you.

But the good part, for me—all the great people I meet and who really seem to love me from just the few weak cracks I make on my wife's shows—well, that's worth a whole lot to me. And when fame swamps me, when I feel overcome by the awesome celebrity it's been my privilege to witness and be part of, well, then, I try to remember the sweet and funny stuff. There's plenty o' that.

Riptide Red Beans and Rice

Paula just loves this recipe. Versions of it are quite popular in the West Indies, where they call it "rice and peas."

PREP TIME: 2½ hours, plus soaking time
SERVES: 4 or 5

1 pound red beans, soaked in about 2 quarts water overnight
1 large smoked ham hock or a ham bone
5 celery ribs, chopped
1 green bell pepper, chopped
1 bay leaf
4 or 5 garlic cloves, minced
1 large onion, chopped
2 tablespoons dried parsley flakes
½ teaspoon cayenne pepper, or to taste
1 teaspoon cumin
1 teaspoon black pepper
1½ to 2 pounds smoked sausage, sliced into 3-inch chunks
Salt
½ cup chopped scallions, both the green and white parts
Cooked white rice, for serving

Rinse and drain the soaked beans; place in a 5- to 6-quart Dutch oven and add about 8 cups of fresh water. Add the ham hock and bring to a boil, then reduce the heat and simmer for about

1½ hours, or until the beans are tender. Stir occasionally. Add the celery, green pepper, bay leaf, garlic, onion, parsley, cayenne, cumin, black pepper, and sausage. Add salt to taste; simmer for about 1 hour, stirring occasionally. Add water as necessary. Just prior to serving add the chopped scallions. Serve over hot long-grain white rice. ⚓

5

Travelin' with Paula

One of our senior citizens was travelin' down the freeway when his car phone rang. Answering, he heard his wife's voice urgently warning him, "Herman, I just heard on the news that there's a car goin' the wrong way on Interstate 77. Please be careful!"

"Heck," answered Herman, "it's not just one car—it's hundreds of 'em!"

We have been to many places, driven on many freeways, and seen many incredible things and we have so much fun wherever we go. I guess we do some stuff that's not really expected, but then that's Paula. Last year she had an interview with a fancy-food editor in a big city and we just happened to be starvin' before our appointment. So we stopped by a White Castle and Paula asks for forty—count 'em, *forty*—White Castle burgers. We go into the editor's office and we're chompin' down one burger after another—and everyone who walks by grabs one as well. So the fancy-food editor simply fell in love with my bride—how could you not?

On our first European trip, we went to Paris, France, and we were havin' a grand time. Paris is just a gorgeous place and Paula let loose in the food capital of the world is a sight to behold.

But my wife, for reasons I couldn't understand at first, was kinda down in the dumps. Now, that ain't Paula. It took about ten minutes to find out why (five minutes longer than usual, when Paula's down in the dumps).

"Paris is for young people," she kept saying. She wanted her kids there so bad, she could hardly look at the Eiffel Tower. She kept tryin' to call 'em. No answer. No call back. That was makin' her nuts.

It just so happened that I understood why no one was picking up that phone. Knowin' Paula as we do, her producer Gordon Elliott had arranged for Paula's sons, Jamie and Bobby, and Jamie's wife, Brooke, to travel to Paris to meet and surprise Paula.

The kids were going to catch us at the top of the Hotel Georges V at the Four Seasons restaurant—one of the most exquisite hotels and restaurants in all the world. The view is incredible, and management had made plans to allow us to eat right up on the very top terrace. It was only the second time in the hotel's history that had been permitted. It was goin' to be so cool!

But Paula'd been tryin' to call her kids all day and she finally said, "Well, dang, they won't answer the phone. I just hope nothin's wrong."

"Well, we're overseas, Paula," I said. "You just can't get phone calls so easy over here." I just kept makin' things up, and she was buyin' every lie I came up with.

At one point, we were outside gaping at Notre Dame and Bobby, Jamie, and Brooke had, by sheer accident, ridden by on one o' those double-decker buses and actually saw us lookin' up at the church.

Would you believe they took pictures of us? Paula woulda just flipped her lid off if she'd'a seen 'em on that bus.

So, finally it was time for dinner. We dressed to the nines, went way up to the top of the hotel, and the maître d' put the two of us at a table set for five. I was afraid that might have blown the surprise, but Paula paid no attention.

What a view—it was overwhelming. How could two country bumpkins from South Georgia end up being treated to such a marvelous sight of Paris? Paula just looked and looked and then—wham—she burst into tears. My Paula is nothing if not a family gal. Her tears were streakin' down her face, smearing her mascara and her makeup somethin' awful.

Finally, she calmed down, and she began smiling and we were telling each other how lucky we were to be experiencing this at our age. Holdin' hands, and huggin' and drinkin' wine—Paula and Michael in Paree. Such luck.

Then we heard a voice. It was kind of a familiar voice but the voice said, *"Bonjour."* That's all—just *Bonjour.* Well, maybe it said, *"Bonjour, y'all."* Hey, I haven't got such a good ear for language but dang if that *bonjour* didn't sound more Savannah than French. My Paula broke out into tears again, and this time they just kept comin'; she sure recognized her child's voice, *bonjour* or no *bonjour.* From around the corner, in strolled Bobby and Jamie and Brooke, and Paula almost jumped out of her skin with joy.

Later on, she told me that she did notice the table was set for five: The view was so spectacular, she simply overlooked the three extra settings.

And the kicker: It had been arranged beforehand that Gordon would film Paula and me in Paris for a Christmas television special so the camerapeople in the distance didn't surprise her. What she didn't expect was the sight of her children showin' up.

"I sure hope y'all got that on film," she said to the producer afterward, "because I sure can't reproduce that incredible moment."

The whole thing was captured for posterity and it did make a spectacular special. It was one of the most fun days I ever had travelin' with Paula.

Sometimes, travelin' doesn't get Paula in the best of moods, but we both know that marriage is a give-and-take.

One of the things Paula just loves to do is gamble, tho' you'll never find her gamblin' away the kitchen sink. Once we were in Vegas, and she was in seventh heaven throwin' down the chips. It occurred to me that there was this spectacular Grand Canyon really nearby, and wouldn't it be great to go see it by helicopter as long as we were in Las Vegas?

Well, my gal didn't cotton to that idea too much.

We ended up taking a helicopter ride through the Grand Canyon and she's hated me for it ever since.

"Paula," I said just when she was knockin' 'em dead at the gaming tables, "we *have* to take a helicopter to the Grand Canyon. You can land right *in* the Grand Canyon and you have lunch in the Grand Canyon and we just *have* to do that."

She said, "Well, I don't wanna do that. I wanna just stay here and gamble."

"Well, we can gamble when we come back," I said. "This is how you make memories, girl."

She may sound crazy as a loon sometimes, but she's a grand sport, my Paula. So we get on this helicopter, and it was really hot—like 117 degrees Fahrenheit. Then they crank it up and the air conditioner dries the sweat off of us. We fly to the really ugly part o' the

Grand Canyon, not the pretty part you see in postcards but actually the first part of the Grand Canyon. They let us out in the 117-degree heat to look at the view (what view?) and I kept lookin' at Paula; she was so mad that I got her out of the cool casino to do this. We happened to land at a picnic table, with rocks all around us. Not the kind you've seen in the postcards, the ones with the beautiful colors o' the Grand Canyon: No, ma'am, this was just plain brown rocks.

Our lunch was water and *Hostess Twinkies.* That was the entire lunch they'd packed for us. Paula was gettin' madder and madder.

So we got back in the helicopter and took off. The pilot had told us before that we were gonna see Hoover Dam. It seemed to me we were headed back, though, so I asked, "Where is Hoover Dam?"

The pilot said, and I am not kiddin', "Oh, I forgot about that."

So we had to turn aroun' to go see Hoover Dam, which was worth the detour. Then we had to land on this other mountain and get out of the helicopter and cut the helicopter off to get even more fuel to get back. Should I mention it hadn't gotten any cooler?

Paula was ready to just strangle me and push me off this mountain.

Finally, we got in the helicopter and went back. And she'd tell ya right now, it was the most sickening thing that she'd ever done.

I keep remindin' her, whenever the subject comes up, "Didn't I tell you, darlin', that's how you make memories?"

"Y'all kin just stick those durn memories you know where," she answers with a grin, now that it's over. "Just point me to the roulette wheel."

Travelin' with Paula is definitely not what I was used to. It's not everybody who gets recognized wherever they go: Big cities, little cities, Paris, Canada, St. Lucia, Puerto Rico; wherever we go, people know us. Imagine that feeling for an old salt like me. They come up and say they love us, and that they watch the show. Especially down South, there's a real strong feeling of family—that we're used to—but to be treated like family anywhere we go . . . well, that's the kind of feeling people have for my Paula, and now it translates to me also.

If I'm to be honest with y'all, there's another downside. I do love to travel with Paula, but that means I pretty much have to leave my own career at home. Sometimes, though, I just have to go back to the ship when Paula's expected to be a thousand miles away. She likes me to be with her all the time, and I love that too—but if you have an important job, and I do, well, we've both got to make compromises.

There's just so durn much good I get from travelin' with my wife, though. I didn't have much experience with fine dining; Paula taught me how to tip people properly and how to know which one was my water glass or my fork or piece of bread and not my dinner neighbor's.

Sometimes we don't get to do what regular normal tourists do. Like when we first went to Paris we would, say, go to the Louvre, and they'd film us outside the museum—but we didn't have time actually to go inside. We saw the outside of Notre Dame in Paris, but we never did get to go inside. That's real frustratin'. In London, we were filmed outside the houses of Parliament, but we'll have to wait till another day to actually go inside. It's kinda like taking a kid to a candy store and not lettin' him in—a little aggravatin' but even just to get to see the outside of these places we only read about is pretty thrilling.

Recently we went to St. Lucia in the West Indies, a beautiful Caribbean island. Although this trip was also taped for Paula's show, *Paula's Home Cooking,* we had plenty of time off when the cameras weren't running just to plain enjoy ourselves taking advantage of the glories of the island. To our surprise, people recognized my wife and surrounded her with such love and beautiful smiles. We went to one of the markets to check out the local produce and noticed that a little girl about eight years old was following us. She started tuggin' on me and tuggin' on me and finally she got up the nerve and asked her question. "'Scuse me, sir," she said, "but is that Paula Deen?"

"Why, yes," I told her. "Would you like to meet her?" You should have seen the child grin. So I walked her over to Paula and Paula, as you might have guessed, gave that little girl the biggest hug and the girl was beside herself with excitement.

"I watch you every day," she said to Paula. "I'm your most biggest fan. I live with my grandmother and we both never let anyone change the channel your show's on. We live right over there—want to see?" So we peeked our heads in the door of the little house and the little girl pointed to the television set. The screen couldn't'a been more than ten inches, and that TV occupied a grand place in the livin' room. We wrote down the little girl's name and we introduced her on *Paula's Home Cookin'* when we returned. I wish I could have been there when she heard her name come right over her television set.

We had a sailboat too, and just because I'm a harbor pilot, they put me at the helm. But I don't really get this sailin' thing. Paula told me she wanted to get up close to see another sailboat. It was the one they'd used in the movie *Pirates of the Caribbean*, and she asked me could I get *real* close? Well, to me close is five feet away; that's how close the tugboats and the ships go, side by side actually, when we're dockin'. So, I said okay, I'd go up real close. Paula said, "Oh, suuuure"—she knew I wasn't any good really with sailboats and she thought my mouth overloaded my butt and that I was braggin' about the gettin'-up-close part.

But, I did it—went up *that* close to this ol' sailin' ship—only fifty feet separated us, actually—and she squealed like a stuck pig and we laughed and laughed and laughed! Anything with Paula usually turns out to be fun.

One of the best times we had in St. Lucia was when Paula and I went ziplinin' through the jungle. The zipliner is like a big ol' cable on pulleys to which a harness like a parachute harness is attached. They put that harness on y'all. They give y'all a helmet. One end of the zipliner is attached to a very tall tree or post at one end of the jungle and the other end is attached to a tree-high post about a half mile away. When you're harnessed into the zipline, you jump off from a little platform that stands where the zipliner is attached, and then you go zinging through the forest at what felt like fifty miles an hour, legs danglin' in the air. You gotta finish the ride—no way to stop in the middle. For Paula to tie onto a cable and go whirling along in the air, alone through a dense jungle canopy, was extremely brave—but she did it! I took it as proof that she's finally conquered her crippling agoraphobia.

Remarkable things happen that you never see on television. For example, I couldn't get over the sight of Dan, the cameraman, just in front of us actually ziplinin' *backward* through the jungle to catch the shots of us ziplinin' the right way—that is, forward. Damn brave cameraman! I wouldna' done it.

Paula and I are on the move so much, sometimes it feels as if we just lay down our hats in one place when we're due in another. People ask me all the time, "Gosh, y'all are on the road so much. Doesn't it get wearisome and old?"

It doesn't. You know, we're not goin' cross-country in a minivan, although that sure has its pleasures. We're not campin' out; we're stayin' in the nicest hotels. The restaurants treat us better than royalty. A lotta times, we're flyin' in a private plane and we can stretch out and it's just like takin' a nap in the hammock at home. So it's difficult for me to complain about our taxing schedule. My mother used to say, "You don't have to look around too far to find someone worse off than you are," so even if it is a grueling schedule, it could be a lot worse.

Here's somethin' else about travelin' with Paula. Fact is—and it took me a long time to get this—soon's we're out of the South, we often have trouble with people not understandin' what we're sayin'. It's like we're speakin' a foreign language or somethin'. Finally, I realized what it was: Everyone else talks funny.

If you don't have a touch of the South in yo' mouth, sometimes you won't understand our diction. So this may be the place to give y'all a guide to proper Southern pronunciation.

The world says:	We say:	As in:
Oil	Awl	My favorite salad dressin' is awl and vinegar.
Wash	Warsh	I really need to warsh the car.
Boss	Bahs	Sure hope my bahs don't far me.
Fire	Far	See above.
Tower	Tahr	Paula and I saw the Eiffel Tahr.
Borrowed	Bard	My pal Buckethead bard my pickup truck.
Dead	Did	The old guy is did.
Light	Lot	The day's almost done; the lot is goin'.
Retired	Retard	What would I ever do if I was retard?

The world says:	We say:	As in:
Rights	Rats	If you're a Southerner, y'all will fight for your rats.
Did y'all hear?	Ju-here	Ju-here I burnt the gooey punkin' pie?
Did you pee?	Jaw-p?	Jaw-p when you went to the bathroom?
Did y'all eat?	Jeet	We are starving. Jeet?
It is	Hit's	Hit's a' gonna rain today.
Do you want?	Dwant	Dwant that last piece of pie?
Sharp, twisted cable	Bob war	Stay away from that bob war fence.
Tool for tightening bolts	Ranch	I left my ranch in the truck.

There are some other things you ought to know about Southerners like Paula and me if you happen to meet us in our travels:

1. A true son or daughter of Savannah never assumes that the car in front with the flashin' light is actually goin' to make a turn.

2. A real Southerner will never curse the little old lady drivin' thirty-five on the highway; he'll just say, "Bless her heart," and go around her.

3. Real Southerners know the difference between "pert near" and "a right far" piece and that just "down the road" can be one mile or forty miles.

4. Real Southerners know that "gimme sugar" don't mean pass the sugar.

5. Iced tea is appropriate for all meals, and you start drinking it when you're two. We do like a little tea with our sugar.

6. You don't *push* buttons—you *mash* 'em.

7. Fried catfish is "the other white meat."

8. *Onced* and *twiced* are words.

9. "That was a sure nuff frog strangler yesterday" doesn't mean the pervert got loose from the pervert place. It means it rained a lot.

10. A possum is a flat animal that sleeps in the middle of the road.

11. We don't need no dang drivers ed. If our mommas say we can drive, we can drive, dag nabbit.

Buoy Biscuits

These biscuits are so light they float!

PREP TIME: About 1 hour, including baking time
MAKES: 24 biscuits

5 cups all-purpose flour, plus additional for the board

3 tablespoons sugar

3 tablespoons baking powder

1 teaspoon baking soda

1 teaspoon salt

1 cup vegetable shortening

One ¼-ounce package *or* 2½ teaspoons active dry yeast

3 tablespoons warm water (105° to 115°F)

2 cups buttermilk

Preheat the oven to 450°F. Grease a baking sheet; set aside.

In a large mixing bowl, sift together the flour, sugar, baking powder, baking soda, and salt. Cut in the shortening (I use my hand) until the mixture resembles small peas; set aside.

Dissolve the yeast in the warm water. Add the yeast and buttermilk to the flour mixture and mix with a fork to make a soft dough. Knead briefly.

Roll out the dough on a floured surface and cut out 24 circles with a biscuit cutter. Place on the baking sheet and bake until puffed and golden, about 10 minutes. ⚓

6

Shoppin' with Paula (also Shoppin' for Paula)

On a business trip, Margie tried shoppin' for a gift for her hus-band, and nothin' seemed right. Finally, she stopped into a li-quor store to buy a bottle of wine for him. As she was drivin' home near Taos, New Mexico, she spotted an elderly Navajo woman slowly walkin' along the dusty road. Margie stopped her car to offer a ride to the woman and with a toothless smile of thanks, she got into the car. Tryin' to make conversation, Margie asked the Navajo woman about her life and family.

Silence.

Finally, the old woman pointed to the liquor store bag on the car floor.

"What's in the bag?" she asked.

Margie saw where she pointed and answered, "It's a bottle of wine. I got it for my husband."

The Navajo woman nodded but didn't speak. Then, with the tribal wisdom of an experienced elder she said, "Good trade."

Just about everything I know about shoppin' came from my wife. For years I shopped alone and thought I also made some pretty good trades, but what did I know? Paula is to shoppin' what oxtails is to good.

Actually, when I met Paula, I already knew how to shop for stuff like fish and boats and cars. I just didn't have the money to pay for the last two items. What I learned about shoppin' for jewelry, particularly diamonds, I learned from my own personal research when the need arose, and it sure arose as soon as I decided to marry that white-haired goddess due to her likin' for diamonds.

So I wasn't so dumb at shoppin' as I always make myself out to be.

Shoppin' for Clothes (and Accessories)

Let me start off with this little-known clothes-shoppin' bombshell you'll only read here: Paula Deen hates dressin' rooms. I don't know why, she just does. If you ever walk into a Savannah department store and you see this pretty, white-haired woman trying on jeans right in the aisle, and it sure looks mighty like that television cook Paula Deen, and you say to yourself how could it be Paula Deen gettin' undressed right in the aisle, dollars to doughnuts it is Paula Deen.

When I first saw her do that, I said, "Paula, what're you *doin'* puttin' on those pants over your clothes? People will think you're shopliftin'."

"I'm just tryin' 'em on," she answered. Then she tried on five other things, right there in the aisle.

It used to embarrass me, but it doesn't anymore. I guess Paula has a phobia of some sort about dressin' rooms, and luckily shyness is not a word she understands. I go shopping with her because we do everything together, but it's not my favorite thing to do.

When it comes to clothes, Paula has classic and simple tastes; she goes for colorful but straight-lined blouses and skirts and pants. But here's the thing: Paula is a returner. She buys 'em fast but she doesn't keep 'em long. She may come home with ten things from a fancy department store, try them on at home, and the next day eight will go back to the returns desk and she heads to Walmart. Funny thing is, she knows what she likes, she knows what looks good on her, she knows she gets a cartful of letters every day from fans who ask where she bought that blue shirt or that red one. But sometimes she sees a great-looking slinky dress on someone like Katie Joel whom she greatly admires. Paula buys a similar slinky dress. Then she gets it home and whammo—back it goes.

Maybe the funniest day I had shopping with Paula was the day she decided to buy high-heeled shoes for some awards show where she had to make a presentation. I forgot which store I was in, but I remember I almost wet myself watchin' her tryin' to walk in those shoes. Paula usually wears the same kind of shoes I do—tennis shoes or flip-flops or, at most, very low heels—and to watch her staggering around in red high heels, stumblin' over everyone and everything—well, I knew she'd never make it up to the stage and across that stage without embarrassin' herself something fierce. Most of the time Paula would just as soon go barefoot, and many's the time we're out at some big party and I notice she's taken her shoes off and they're under the table somewhere. 'Course I'm the one who has to go find 'em.

When we go shoppin' for me, it's a different story. I go into a store, knowin' exactly what I want. I say, "Okay, I'll take this and that," and I'm done. Hardly ever even have to try anything on; I know my size.

I'm pretty good at buyin' my own clothes but when we first met, Paula wanted to get rid o' all my old clothes. Bad news. For one thing, she was buyin' turtlenecks for me. Look, my neck is huge. I do not do well in a turtleneck; I look real goofy. Paula would also buy me linen pants, which I like, but they're not me.

I asked her, "What's up with women? You fall in love with somebody and the first thing you do is try to change everythin' that you love about them. And then, all of a sudden, you have somebody else!"

So we agreed I'd go back to wearing what I wanna wear.

My uniform when I met Paula was jeans and T-shirts, and it still is. I had some nice clothes, but not many. Once I had to go to this father-and-daughter dance with Michelle and I didn't have a jacket to wear. I had to run out to the store after work and I found the only gay guy in the world with no sense of style.

He sold me a burgundy jacket, a pair of slacks, and a tie. Were you listenin'? The color of the jacket was *burgundy*.

Well, I wore that burgundy jacket to the dance, and afterward, I wore it everywhere: weddin's, funerals, Easter Sunday services.

One day, a guy at work told me I looked like an aluminum sidin' salesman in the jacket. After I met Paula and she helped me to start buyin' better stuff, everybody I knew came up to us and told me, "Thank God y'all got rid of that burgundy jacket."

Tell you a funny story about shoppin' for clothes with Paula in an unlikely place. This is actually the story of a disaster of an evening.

We were going to a cocktail party at Wolfgang Puck's restaurant in L.A. Paula was a rising star at the Food Network, so we were all supposed to be on our best behavior. I carried Paula's stuff to the plane and I had a hang-up bag for my clothes—which I forgot to bring. I just left that bag at home. Biggest party of my life, and I left my damn clothes home.

We got to L.A., where we were about to try to impress people, and I had all o' Paula's stuff and no clothes for me.

I knew I somehow had to buy a jacket to wear with the pants and shirt. But it was a Sunday—all the stores were closed. Even if they were open, I'm not built like most people—I can't buy a suit or sport jacket off the rack and we had only two hours to get to the party. No time for alterations.

How am I gonna pull this one off? I thought.

We left Paula's stuff at the Four Seasons Hotel, jumped into a cab, and asked the driver to take us to the nearest Goodwill store. Sure enough, Paula spotted a nice enough jacket on the rack (she said it was a double knit) in just my size. It would have to do. Actually, it wasn't bad at all. Fifteen bucks and we were off to Wolfgang Puck's restaurant, Spago. I figured I'd pass it off as cashmere if anyone asked. No one asked.

We get to the party. I fill up on hors d'oeuvres and as I'm sitting down to dinner, I immediately spill my champagne flute all over the fancy tablecloth and every plate within reach. Those flutes are top-heavy, if you ask me. They had to change the whole tablecloth. I was the center of attention.

I asked for a Diet Coke; wasn't goin' to fool with those skinny champagne glasses anymore.

A waiter brought the Coke and set it down. I turn around a great crab dish they've brought me for dinner so Paula can reach it and taste it, and whoops—I knock over the Diet Coke just in case I haven't brought enough attention to myself. This time they don't bother to change the whole cloth; they just set down a huge napkin over the stain in front o' me.

Paula was appalled.

I got better at social functions and we never did have to shop at a Goodwill again. Thank the Lord.

•   •   •

Look at me—do I look like the kind of guy who would shop for a damn purse? No? That's what I hoped y'all would say.

One day, we were rushin' to catch another plane, this time to Chicago, and Paula asked if she gave me a big check she'd just received. She just *knew* she'd given it to me to hold. I just *knew* she hadn't. My pockets were crammed with all her other stuff—gum, ChapStick, fingernail filers . . . I'd never have put a check in there.

We made a few phone calls and located the check.

But before we found it, I'd made a decision then and there.

It was time for my first man-purse. I'd seen them on yuppies, and it gradually come to me that this ain't a stupid invention. You can carry all your credentials, your wallet, your passport, the check your wife hands you at the last minute—and you don't stretch out your pockets. Paula marches me into a store at the mall ten minutes after we land in Chicago and I buy my first man-purse. I was a little intimidated and embarrassed about carrying it at first, but now not at all.

A man-purse doesn't take away from manliness. Now I'm happy to report, I have four man-purses. Count 'em—f o u r.

I don't hardly go anywhere anymore without my man-purse.

Got somethin' to say about that?

Shoppin' for Fish

Now, let me get to somethin' I do know a lot about—shoppin' for seafood. When you're buyin' seafood, you use three of your natural senses: You look at it, you smell it, you touch it.

The biggest clue to freshness in fish products is smell. Don't hesitate to smell your crab, fish, shrimp, or oysters, and if there's a strong, well . . . pungently fishy smell and if you can smell your seafood before you even see it, you don't wanna mess with it.

Buyin' raw shrimp? If their tails are black or tightly curled, that means that they're gettin' close. Either they're old or they've been in the freezer for a long while.

Oysters? If an oyster's open and you know it opened all by itself, y'all never want to eat that oyster. Throw it away. It opened when it naturally died and it could have died a month ago; same with clams. They should open only when they get steamed open in your pot.

Buyin' fish? Look at the eyes. If they're bright and clear, that's good. If they're dull, clouded over, or milky, that's bad. Those are old eyes on an old fish. In that way, fish are a lot like people.

Touch counts, too. Fish get mushy when they're not all that fresh, so if you press your finger on the flesh of the fish and it feels very soft and pulpy that means it's bad or old. The flesh should be firm and it should spring right back after you press it.

The best tip I can give you on freezin' fresh fish or shrimp is to keep air away from it. When I am goin' to put shrimp in the freezer, I will get containers and fill them up with the shrimp, then cover the shrimp with water. That removes all the air and the shrimp won't get freezer burn. After you defrost the shrimp, you just pour out the water.

The best way to freeze cleaned and picked crab is to put it into a plastic container, cover it with milk, then freeze it. That keeps it fresh. It's especially good if you're usin' the crab to make crab stew. It wasn't Paula's way until I taught her better.

Of course you can go ahead, catch the crabs, pick the crabs, make the deviled crabs, and freeze 'em. But just remember, if the freezer goes on the blink for just a little while or if it's accidentally been left open for a few hours, it's time to start cryin'. Those crab cakes or deviled crabs will go bad. Throw them away even though you put a lot of work in 'em.

Some people feel you can't successfully freeze any fish but if you carefully gut 'em, clean 'em, and cut off their heads—I don't like my food lookin' at me when I eat it—they freeze well. If you fillet them, fish also freeze nicely. It's a good idea to date what you put in your freezer. Almost everyone forgets to do that.

It's been my experience that although there are exceptions, most supermarkets or fish markets don't sell spoiled fish or seafood for the simple reason that they don't want anythin' smellin' up their stores. And bad fish will definitely do that.

Never cook a dead lobster, a dead crab, an opened clam, or an opened oyster. Throw him away. Or her.

Shoppin' for Meat

We have a great butcher at Publix grocery store and he'll cut almost anything for us. Paula and I like rib eye steaks best. There's a lot more marbling (that's a butcher's way of sayin' fat) in it and that makes it taste better. 'Course, if you're health conscious, eat skirt or flank steak. They've got less fat in them, and less flavor, I think.

You don't have to buy the steak or chopped meat or chops that's lying there on the shelves in your market. Make friends with the butcher and he'll cut the best parts of the beef or pork fresh, just for you. Great butchering is almost a dying art. A lot of the product from especially large grocery stores now comes straight from the factory, already cut and prepackaged.

But if you know the butcher, he'll do right by you. I love to shop with Paula because naturally she flirts with the butcher and gets the best cuts. We almost always go home with some oxtails, which we call "swingin' sirloin."

Oxtails taste almost like a beef stew or short ribs, but they're more tender, especially when they're in a soup. I think it's the cartilage in the tail that makes it tender. The stickier the oxtails, the better the eatin'.

I particularly like to shop for pork ribs. That's probably because I just love the art of cookin' on a grill and the crowd of family it draws.

Sometimes what looks good or what's on sale determines the cut I buy. It might be the regular rib slabs, the baby backs, or just a good ol' country-style cut. Regardless, they're all delicious.

Before I cook my ribs, I rub them with Paula's butt rub seasoning, pour a little vinegar over them, and let them marinate for from four hours to overnight. Then I cook 'em on the grill or in the oven. The great thing about ribs is that you can precook 'em at 250 degrees Fahrenheit in the oven and just finish 'em up on the grill. Just make sure you cover them with foil if you're cookin' in the oven. The last ten or fifteen minutes on the grill, I swab them with my favorite barbecue sauce, Paula Deen BBQ Sauce.

I have a grill that works with indirect heat; it's called a Sikes Cooker. The fire's on one side and the meat's on the other, and it's just terrific because the cooking fat never causes flare-ups. That's one fine-ass grill, y'all.

Shoppin' for Fruit and Vegetables

Shoppin' for vegetables is almost like shoppin' for fish. You have to use your sight, touch, and smell. Tomatoes should feel firm, not mushy. They don't have to be bright red unless you want 'em for that day; tomatoes ripen very fast.

To select a ripe cantaloupe, pick it up and smell it; it should smell sweet. Then press on one end firmly with your thumb. If it's soft to the touch, it's ready to eat. Oh, yeah—you press on the *stem* end of the fruit. And it should not feel mushy elsewhere on the fruit, just firm.

For a honeydew melon, gently shake it; if you hear the seeds movin' around inside, it's ready to serve.

Don't buy a brown or very spotted banana. Better to buy them green because they ripen so fast. I can remember when we were kids, my mother would always have green tomatoes or bananas sittin' on the windowsill, waitin' for the sun's warmth and the ripenin'.

The green veggies? You can hardly go wrong no matter what you buy. Just make sure the green ain't brown.

Shoppin' for Vehicles

Paula and I shop together for almost everythin' we buy, except maybe cars, boats, and Jet Skis. She's not so great at shoppin' for those. Paula's interested in comfortable transportation. Period. She can't tell the difference between a Mercedes and a Toyota, and she doesn't care. As long as it has a radio, a gas pedal, a brake, and an air conditioner, she's okay with the car. Boats, she has no opinion on. Ditto Jet Skis.

On the other hand, I want a drivin' machine that's safe; it has to have done well in crash tests. Such vehicles have better resale value. I research these things but I must admit I also like cool-looking vehicles of every kind. I love speed.

Paula doesn't care beans about speed.

For these reasons, I rarely go boat, car, or Jet Ski shoppin' with Paula and that's why this is a short section.

Shoppin' for Presents for People

You know, when we go on a trip, we try to bring back presents for everybody. I think it's gettin' to the point where it might be easier to give 'em a check and tell 'em to buy what they want. But here are some points I find useful:

If you go to a place like France, you want to bring home a gift that says MADE IN FRANCE, like French pottery or a French sweater. People like that.

I've taken to shopping on the Web, especially for holidays like Christmas, because it's so much easier and you can just get stuff delivered to the house. If you do that, I think you should also do a little research and not just give people your credit card, not knowin' who you're dealin' with. You could look up a company on the Web, get reviews on the companies, and then make your decision. Make sure you're on a secure Web site before you start handin' credit cards out. And always get a confirmation number and a confirmation page so you can track your purchase. By the way, I like to buy stuff in multiples.

Paula's very good at choosing the perfect present. She hunts 'em up in markets, in little antique shops, and in regular department stores and everyone is usually delighted with the personal-type unusual stuff she chooses. I don't have the patience she has.

The only place Paula ever screws up majorly is when she's shoppin' for a present for her niece Corrie.

Corrie is fabulously beautiful and always put together. I might add she has fabulously expensive taste, to say the least.

So, this past Christmas, Paula was in Philadelphia on the way to appear on QVC. Lo and behold, when she got to the studio, they were havin' a shoe sale in the warehouse and all these very fine shoes were selling for five and ten dollars a pair. Even better, the proceeds were goin' to fight breast cancer.

Paula went berserk! She bought that child twenty, yes I said twenty, pairs of shoes just knowin' that Corrie would adore every one.

Christmas came and Paula was just beamin' about all those shoes.

Well, Corrie really tried to be gracious that Christmas mornin', but I have to tell y'all that all twenty pairs of those shoes are in our garage in trash bags waiting for the Goodwill truck. Why? I'm not really sure. Maybe it was something about them bein' the wrong size?

Still, Paula's got a great eye; she can find stuff that looks like junk and we can fix it up so it looks perfect. But I've always done that. I used to go with my mother to garage sales years ago. You know, you can almost look at these antique stores as a way of unearthing history. I've heard of a guy who bought a picture from an antique shop just to get the frame because he didn't like the picture at all. When he took the picture out, behind the glass and tucked into the frame, he found the best preserved copy of the Declaration of Independence. And it sold for like two million dollars. You can't expect to find the Declaration of Independence, but you can definitely find a piece of ancient gold or something like that.

I know sometimes I've embarrassed Paula a little bit by tryin' to talk to some of the store owners and bargain a little bit to git the price down, but she always says, "You're embarrassin' me." And I always say, "Well, go outside."

Anyhow, I work with the owners and most o' the time they'll work with ya. You know, I want to give somebody a fair price, but I also know there's a markup . . . so I figure they'll take a little less of a markup. You know, if they can't do it, they'll say no. I've been told no more than once, so I'm not embarrassed to ask. Haggling is a game. You do it with respect for the seller.

One time, Paula had gone outside after I started bargaining with a dealer and I told her, "Well, the good news is, the guy took my offer. The bad news is, the guy took my offer. Now I can't haggle anymore."

Shoppin' for Coffee

I really like good coffee. Ships I dock come in from all over the world so I'm always bein' offered a cup o' coffee from Costa Rica, Italy, Colombia, Greece, and a dozen other places that are known for good coffee. I must say I've become a coffee connoisseur. One time, a ship from Colombia came in and when I went aboard to dock, the captain asked me what I wanted to drink. I said "Coffee. Milk. One sugar." He brought me a glass of milk and some sugar—totally missed the coffee. I knew he was thinking, *No wonder the guy's so fat; he drinks milk with sugar in it.*

If I'm pickin' my favorite beans, they'll probably be a Costa Rican and Colombian mix. Any Colombian blend is just wonderful—full-bodied, and strong, strong, strong. I enjoy grindin' the beans, but I also like the already ground product and I like it all so much, I've even just gone into the business, callin' it Captain Michael's Coffees. Paula sells it on her Web site and it's also now in a few local supermarkets.

My favorite from all the blends I make is called Captain's Choice, naturally. I take it with a dash of milk and an envelope of Splenda.

Paula loves the flavored coffees, so I've got one called Paula Deen's Hazelnut Rum Cake and damned if it doesn't taste exactly like her cake. She loves the Double Chocolate flavor, too.

Shopping *for* Paula

I knew I was gonna buy Paula a diamond ring for our engagement and I wanted to find out how to get a really good one. I did some major research. This is what I learned. Follow me along now if you're anywhere close to buying bling.

If You're Goin' for the Diamond . . .

Either shop with a really knowledgeable jewelry person or buy what you like on approval, which means after you have it professionally appraised, you can return it if the diamond doesn't meet your expectations.

There are four things you have to know about shoppin' for real diamonds and they're known as the four Cs.

COLOR: The best and rarest, almost impossible-to-find diamonds are truly colorless or what are called "white" diamonds. You probably can't afford these unless you have a name that rhymes with Crump or Mockerfeller.

What you may be able to afford will be the nearly colorless diamond, a terrific stone; a faintly tinted diamond, which usually means just a little yellowish; a lightly tinted, quite yellowish; and the very tinted, which are so yellow, they're almost brown. Don't go there. Give her a sapphire or an opal instead of a lousy diamond. By the way, don't confuse a yellowish diamond with a canary diamond, which is quite extraordinary.

Try to buy your diamond as a loose stone before it's mounted as a ring. Once a diamond is set into metal, the color can seem to change, which means a slightly tinted stone can appear almost white and colorless when mounted in a white setting of platinum or white gold. On the other hand, mounting a diamond in a gold setting will usually make the tone seem more yellow.

Sounds pretty damn professional, right? When Captain Michael learns, he learns.

CLARITY: The clarity of a stone refers to how "clean" it is. Some stones have trace minerals, scratches, or other blemishes, which can usually be seen only through a special magnifying glass. Interestingly, the clarity of the stone doesn't have much of an effect on its brilliance except in huge diamonds like the famous Hope Diamond. If the stone you're lookin' at is what they call "eye-clean" (that is, you can't see imperfections without a magnifying glass), imperfections won't make it less fiery. Of course the higher its clarity, the more valuable a diamond is, but most stones have at least a trace of imperfections in them that don't show at all or show only if you're really looking and really eagle-eyed.

CUT: Cut is probably the most important of the four Cs. The cut does not refer to the shape of the diamond, which can be round, square, oblong, oval, and even heart-shaped. It refers to how the depth and width *within* the stone are cut.

Some people say things to Paula like, "Your diamond has so much life, so much fire." Well, the diamond cutter helped to give it that life and fire. The way a stone is cut determines how beautifully the light will shine into and out of the surface and depth of the diamond. Even if a diamond measures up in every other way, a poor cut can make it look dull because the light does not travel well into and out of the stone to show off its best qualities.

CARAT: Finally, how big is this baby? The carats determine how much it weighs. In the diamond business, size isn't everything. A beautiful, only slightly flawed small stone is considered by most experts to be much more valuable than a humongous yellowish stone.

You know, I think you should have a relationship with your jeweler. It's not a great idea to go to someone you don't know from Adam and say, "Gimme a two-carat diamond and gimme a pretty one." Because that's not gonna work.

So go to a jeweler you trust. Then have the stone appraised by an expert. Then pick out your settin'. I've always liked platinum, which is a little more expensive than white gold. I read somewhere that all the platinum that's ever been mined in the world can fit in the average-size livin' room. That gives you an idea of why platinum is more expensive.

I use three jewelers especially: Levy Jewelers in Savannah, another one on De Rene Street called A & E Jewelry, and a guy named Michael Ross from Mobile, Alabama. I can call any of 'em and say, "What do you have that Paula would like?" and be sent the perfect piece for me to look at. If I don't like it, I send it back. You can do the same thing with a dealer when you've built up trust. After I do that, I can drop Paula's rings off for any adjustment and I don't have to worry 'bout 'em exchangin' diamonds or messin' with the stones in any way. A dishonest jeweler can take out your good stones and then take an inferior diamond and put it in your setting and you'll never know the difference till you go to sell it. It looks like yours, but it isn't.

Just like it's a good idea to know your butcher or your fish store guy, you have to know your jeweler. That is, if you have a partner who likes pretty jewelry.

And I do.

The final words I have for y'all on buying jewelry for a loved person:

Buy what *you* like. She'll like it too, and she'll always remember the day you gave it to her.

I like pretty jewelry on women. Maybe it's just that I like women and the jewelry enhances the woman. Bottom line: Long as I can, I'll keep buyin' it for my gal.

Shoppin' for a Christmas Tree

There's an item Paula and I just love to shop for together at Christmastime: the tree.

Paula's very particular. Our Christmas tree was probably the first thing we shopped for together when we first met. Paula said that nobody in her family would go with her because she was such a stickler. She would inspect every single tree so carefully, you'd think she was buyin' diamonds.

Well, we bought what we thought was the perfect tree but once we got it home, we realized that it didn't have a back to it. Didn't have a damn back! Paula said she was blinded by love, that's how she was fooled. Well, I had to cut off limbs from another tree and tie and wire 'em to our tree to make it look like a full tree. By the time Christmas came around, most of the needles had fallen off my poorly constructed Christmas tree. But Paula just laughed her great laugh and said she didn't care; she was just so excited to be sharing Christmas together, needles on the floor or not.

So my first advice to y'all when shoppin' for a Christmas tree is to walk around it. Make sure that the tree is a tree all around. Look for green needles, which means the tree is fresh. Brown needles will fall out before you've finished the ham. If you can pull out the needles, even though they're still green, the tree won't last through the holiday.

You gotta cut the bottom off when you get home, and then put the tree in a bucket of water for a couple of hours or overnight to soak up as much water as possible.

You know, I do like a pretty tree as much as anyone else, but I think it's more important than its bigness or greenness to know who's sellin' this tree. I love to get trees that are sold by the Boy Scouts or the Girl Scouts or another worthy organization. I'd rather buy a not-so-perfect tree from the Boy Scouts than the Rockefeller Center tree from Home Depot, although I have nothin' against Home Depot. Paula agrees with me totally on this one.

Jodi's Famous Seafarin' Squash Casserole

If you like squash, you'll clamor for more of this casserole!
This is my sister-in-law Jodi Groover's recipe.

PREPARATION TIME: About 1 hour, including cooking time
SERVES: 4 to 6

2 tablespoons unsalted butter
2 tablespoons flour
1 cup milk
8 saltine crackers, crushed
2 cups mashed cooked yellow squash
1 cup grated Cheddar cheese
1 egg, lightly beaten
½ teaspoon salt

Preheat the oven to 350°F. Grease an 8-inch square baking pan.

In a saucepan over medium heat, melt the butter. Slowly stir in the flour and cook, stirring, for 2 to 3 minutes. Add the milk, then cook the mixture, stirring constantly, until thick. Stir in the crackers, then the squash. Stir the cheese, egg, and salt into the squash mixture. Pour into the prepared pan and bake for 30 minutes. ⚓

7

Eatin' with Paula—
Cookin' Too, Y'all

Two delicate flowers of Southern womanhood were conversing on the porch swing of a large white pillared mansion.

The lady from Alabama said, "When my first child was born, my husband built this beautiful mansion for me."

The Georgia peach said, "Well, isn't that nice."

The first woman continued, "When my second child was born, my husband bought me this fine Cadillac."

Again the Georgia peach said, "Well, isn't that nice."

The Alabama belle went on, "Then, when my third child was born, my husband gave me this gorgeous diamond bracelet."

The Georgia peach once again said, "Well, isn't that nice."

The first woman said, "Well, what did your husband do for you when your first child was born?"

"My husband sent me to charm school," declared the Georgia peach.

> *"Charm school?" exclaimed the Alabama belle. "Land sakes,*
> *child, what on earth for?"*
>
> *The Georgia peach responded, "So that instead of saying,*
> *'Who gives a shit?' I learned to say, 'Well, isn't that nice.'"*

Every Southerner with charm and smarts knows that tomatoes, along with eggs, bacon, grits, and coffee, are the berries when it comes to breakfast, and that redeye gravy and country ham is also a breakfast food.

Paula knows it best but I'm still the better cook, although the world doesn't know *that* yet. I remember one time we had been on the road and Paula was starving for our kind of food. "Michael," she said, "I'm just cravin' some chicken and dumplin's. I'm gonna give myself thirty minutes to make 'em."

Paula made her chicken 'n' dumplin's.

I ate 'em.

"How do you like them, darlin'?" she asked.

"You know, they're pretty good," I told her.

"Whaddya mean, *pretty good*? You don't like them, do ya?"

"No, they're very good, but mine are better," I told her.

That did it.

"Well, why don' chu git up off your fat ass and make me some, then?" she asked.

Well, I didn't. It wasn't worth it. And I didn't have the time that day. I cook a lot slower than Paula does. She says I'm like a tortoise behind a stove, that you could almost starve to death before I get finished preparing a meal. That may be, but when I'm done, you better believe everything's just delicious, *especially* the chicken 'n' dumplin's. Hers aren't bad by any means, but I put celery stalks in mine. I take the chicken off the bones and the little veins out o' the chicken; a lot more work goes into mine than Paula's. Paula just throws the cleaned chicken and the spices in and cooks.

She uses more spices in general than I do anyway. I hardly ever salt anything unless it's something like grits (there's a law that says you have to salt grits) and corn on the cob and French fries when they come to the table. But Paula—I've seen her put salt in beer and on watermelon.

Okay, okay—kiddin' aside, trying to learn from watchin' that gal is like takin' batting lessons from Hank Aaron. You can watch all you want, but it'll never be the same, much as I like to rib her. Paula owns—I don't know how many—cookbooks but very seldom will she pull out one.

You've just got to watch how she measures things to really understand. I've seen the best tugboat cooks do the same thing. They use their hands, not spoons or measures. They know just how much is needed—a teaspoon, a tablespoon—but the hand of a true chef knows better than a spoon. Paula does the same thing. She can taste a spoonful of liquid from a giant pot of stuff and just know what's going on in the rest of that pot. Ninety-five percent of everyone else would just eat the soup and not notice it was too salty till they got thirsty later on. Her palate is so developed she can tell in one tiny taste what's going on in the whole mess.

Tugboat cooks have different needs from Paula's and on boats is where I learned my cookin'. In heavy seas, for example, you got to put down wet power towels and put any plates or pots on top of them so they don't go slipping off the counter. They have racks on top of the stove to keep pots and pans from slidin' around. It's just a different game from cookin' on dry land.

I remember the first meal I ever cooked on a boat. I was just a kid and workin' on a tugboat called the *Royal Endeavor*. I'll never forget, the captain's name was Millard Williams, and one morning Captain

Williams told me to go fix breakfast. Well, I was a deckhand, and I reminded him, "Captain Williams—I'm not real good at cookin'."

He says, "Well, just go try."

So I said, "Okay, whaddya want?"

He says, "Eggs, ham, grits, coffee, and toast."

So I went downstairs and put the grits on, and I clean forgot to salt 'em. If you don't salt grits to start with, they're terrible. They're horrible. They're inedible. Captain Williams said he wanted some ham and eggs, so I looked for the ham. Well, in the refrigerator, there was luncheon meat ham. So I put that in the fryin' pan and fried it up with some eggs.

What I didn't know was there's a preservative in luncheon meat ham that makes it real sticky when fried. It even makes the pan disgustingly sticky. When I fried the luncheon meat ham up, it also shrank down to about the size of a playin' card.

Well, I put that on the plate anyway. I was in a hurry, so instead o' cleanin' my pan up, I started to fry my eggs in the same pan as the luncheon meat. The black gunk that come outta the luncheon meat ham was still in the fryin' pan, but I wasn't interested in the niceties of frying. I just wanted to get the captain his breakfast.

Well, when I tried to turn the eggs over, they just sat there, stuck to the pan, lookin' repulsive. What could I do? I put 'em on the plate along with the saltless grits. Next, I made the coffee. I wasn't real bad at coffee, but I wasn't real good either. And the toast. Toast was my specialty. It came out just perfect.

So I carried it all upstairs to the captain.

He said, "What is this?"

I said, "That's breakfast."

He didn't even taste it, just rolled the window down, threw the plate and everything on it overboard, and said, "I'm not eatin' that, Michael."

And I had to say, "Well, I don't blame ya, I wouldn't eat it either."

After a while, as I watched the real cook, I learned. I got good at cookin', especially one-pot wonders like beef stew or chicken 'n' dumplin's.

Eatin' at home with Paula is different from what y'all see on television. We kind of have these rituals. Like I always get the coffee first thing in the morning for both of us. We drink it either in bed or on our porch—anywhere we can watch the dolphins jump in the creek out our window. And I make the ice cream—Paula says I make it better than anyone, even her. But Paula does almost everything else if it's not made outdoors on a grill; that's my specialty.

If truth be told, when I met Paula, I had just about quit cookin'. When she came into my life I thought, *Woo hoo! I'm goin' to be able to let someone else worry about the stove, now I've got a pro in that department.*

But we still talk a lot about cookin' and eatin' and we think about it too. Almost everything takes place over a meal. The best plans are made over oxtails, my favorite. There's verbal lovemakin' to be made over a meal. Kissin' ain't far from smackin' your lips in appreciation of a good pie. Rarely but when necessary, there's arguing to be accomplished over a good meal; it softens the argument somehow. And even dyin' is accompanied by good eats. Our Southern funeral food is the best in the world. Everybody waits to see what's comin' from Paula's stove to a house of bereavement, strange as that sounds.

I don't think there's a Southerner alive or dead who doesn't have a special appreciation for food. Take Elvis Presley, for example. Now, the King knew how to eat. He loved his pork chops, his meat and potatoes, his fried chicken, his gravy with white bread, and his banana puddin', just like us. Elvis's favorite snack was fried peanut butter and banana sandwiches. Paula did get to one of his concerts but they never met, nor did he ever get to taste a Paula Deen fried cup-cake, but if he did, he would have thought twice about Priscilla. I've heard ol' Elvis thought milk made you sexy. To each his own. Paula and I got other, better sexy-makin' foods. Caramel, anyone?

When Paula and I first dated, she was wise enough to make me a seven-layer caramel cake. The layers of caramel frostin' were almost as thick as the cake layers. With each slice of that cake, my knees grew weaker. Love was in the air, or maybe in the caramel. It was just an incredible taste sensation. Frankly, I believe she sealed the deal right then with that caramel layer cake, although I never said so at the time.

Actually, when it comes to cookin', one of the reasons I think I love Paula's cookin' so much is because she cooks like my momma used to cook. That means a lot o' food. My momma would fry chicken for . . . lessee . . . It was my two brothers, my father, and my grandfather, and my mother, and myself. Momma would fry up three chickens for us. She would eat two little wings and we would eat the rest. She always had a pot on the stove, just like my wife.

Fresh food was a big thing with my momma. When I was small, we had a garden, so we always had fresh tomatoes, fresh cucumbers, fresh green beans, and fresh butter beans. Momma would can what we didn't eat so we'd have food year-round. We raised animals, too, so we would always have fresh meat, and we were always fishin' or crabbin', so we always had fresh seafood. We ate well. Times are different now, so when Paula and I eat at home, we're not eatin' on the level of freshness we ate when I was comin' up. And because Paula is so wildly busy, she has very little time to really do much cookin' herself. I'm not a difficult husband when it comes to feedin' me. I really like most everything. But wait—maybe I'm lying.

Don't give me brussels sprouts, I don't like 'em at all. That's pretty strange, because I like cabbage. And I'm not real crazy about carrots, which I'll eat maybe in beef stew, but never when Paula makes 'em all by themselves for us.

I really can't complain because eatin' in my home always pretty much means you're eatin' good; the cook does right.

Listen, everyone has a bad day sometimes, even Paula Deen. One time, we had some oysters I'd just collected and Paula said, "Would you like some oyster stew?"

I said, "Yeah, I'm really hungry."

So she stopped by the store and got some milk in a little pint container. It happened to be vanilla-flavored milk, but neither of us noticed it at the time. Even if I did, I prob'ly wouldna' mentioned it. Who am I to tell Paula Deen how to cook anything?

So she made the oyster stew with the vanilla-flavored milk and gave me the biggest bowl. As I was tastin' it, she said, "How is it?"

I said, "Well, it tastes sweet, like a milkshake. What happened, what'd you do, what'd you put in it, sugar or somethin'?"

"Nothin'," she said, "only the milk and the butter like I always do. You're pretty fussy with your special oysters, ain't you, Michael?"

It must have been a flavored butter or somethin', I thought.

"Just taste it," I said to her, "and tell me what a pro thinks."

"Oh, God, what is it?" she yelped.

So we looked and looked and finally noticed that the milk was vanilla-flavored. It was like an oyster milkshake we were eatin.' Disgustin'.

Paula has a phrase she uses that's printed all over the aprons sold in her store: COUNTRY COOKIN' MAKES YOU GOOD LOOKIN'. Well, I don't know about the good-lookin' part, but it'll sure make ya fat if you eat it exclusively. Unless you flavor your oysters with vanilla. Then you'll never get fat.

We eat out at a lot of restaurants because we're always on the go. When we go into a restaurant and they recognize Paula, they pull out all the stops; Paula don't love that too much. For me, it's awful nice, but almost a curse in some ways. If you and I go to a restaurant in Savannah and we each order ten shrimp, they'll bring you the ten and bring me twenty. Everyone wants to impress the Deen gal (and now the Groover guy) and the buzz goes through the restaurant the moment we set foot in. The chefs all march out to say hello to Paula and me and the pastry chef's already started his best specialty back in the kitchen. If I'm watching my weight, I always say no dessert, but fat chance of that: They think I can't make up my mind, so they bring me one of everything and I end up with eight desserts.

But here's the neatest thing that happens in restaurants: Sometimes we two will just walk into a place and I'll tell them we don't want to order off the menu; just feed us what you want 'cause we're dying of hunger. That's when we get the best of the best and it's a neat way to eat because you'd never think of half the things they trot out. You just know that with Paula Deen sittin' near me, even if she doesn't say a word, they're not goin' to bring her anything but top-shelf stuff.

Recently we were doin' a photo shoot for Paula's magazine, *Cooking with Paula Deen,* in the Chesapeake Bay region of Maryland. We and the whole crew—about thirty of us—went out for dinner to the Crab Claw, a salty little restaurant on the water in St. Michael's. Every manner of seafood just kept comin' to the table, courtesy of the owners, a feisty eighty-two-year-old woman and her daughter. There were delicious steamers and shrimp and crab claws and soft-shelled crabs and oysters and lobster and you name it. We were in heaven and stuffed to the gills. When it came time to pay the bill, there was no bill. The owners said they were so pleased to host Paula, they simply wouldn't charge us. Imagine that!

Sometimes it's hardest to eat in Paula's own restaurant, The Lady & Sons. So many people travel to Savannah and they actually plan

At least they didn't put me on
a bearskin!

That horse doesn't look too
happy carryin' both of us
big boys.

Big brother Hank and me with
our mother and father.

Merry Christmas, everyone!

About the only time you could
get me in a tie was for my
school picture.

One of the last pictures of me
without my beard!

I was always a real hands-on dad.

From left to right: Aunt Dottie and Aunt Mary (my mother's sisters), first cousin once removed Cindy, my mother, Hank, me, and Nick.

Michelle and Anthony—all grown up now.

My beautiful daughter,
Michelle.

At work, where I love to be.

On my wedding day, in front of Bethesda Chapel.

With my bride.

We clean up real nice!

The day Paula got to ring the opening bell at the New York Stock Exchange.

Sailin' ain't the only way to travel.

Whether it's work or fun, I love bein' on the water.

My side of our extended family: Michelle's husband, Daniel Reed; Michelle; Anthony's girlfriend, Jennifer Moesch; Anthony.

The boys and Brooke surprised Paula at dinner on top of the Hotel George V in Paris.

Settin' up for a TV shoot in our backyard. Gotta be the world's shortest commute!

Sometimes we just like to be tourists.

Who says romance is only for the young?

their vacation around eatin' at the restaurant in hopes o' meetin' Paula. So if we show up, Paula cannot be rude. And she's not. But the line outside the restaurant is gridlocked when she's around because many people in the restaurant get up from their seats to chat and kid with her and hug her. They're not eatin' and not orderin'; they're just talkin' to Paula. Nobody leaves. It's kinda like Mickey Mouse comes to the park and you want to take home a piece of Mickey.

People wanna go over and talk to her and tell her their stories because everybody has a story. Somebody in their family has overcome some kinda obstacle just like Paula has. She wants to listen but really can't, not to every story. So we occasionally just go down to the store that's next door to the restaurant, because even before she goes in the restaurant, that line outside (which moves slowly anyway) just stops when they see her. That's not so good for business and not so good for the people waiting in the line.

The truth? Bein' part of the show doesn't bother me even a little bit. You know, you can't be famous and not be approachable. At least we can't. So that's the price you pay. And Paula truly loves her fans.

So I've learned how to eat in a special way when this happens, or else, believe me, I'd be down to a hundred pounds. When someone comes over to our table to talk to Paula, I'm usually in the middle between the person and Paula. I make my welcoming sounds, then get down to the business of consumin' my dinner, 'cause at that point it ain't me the guest is interested in and it's the meal I'm most interested in.

There's an eatin' method I developed: I scoop my food up on my fork, then I come down with my fork, practically to my lap, and let the guests make their eye contact with my wife without my fork filled with fried chicken gettin' in the way. Then I'll watch for the opportunity when the people are not yet aimin' that camera at her. At that moment, I will bring *up* that fork while my food is still warm, and shove it in my mouth. That way, I don't ruin any pictures or stop the eye contact. And I can continue to eat while my food is still warm.

Livin' with Paula's an art form. It tests your ingenuity.

I have to keep rememberin' that eatin' or drinkin' with Paula is marvelous, but sometimes it can be a challenge. Once Paula took me to a food and wine festival in Orlando, Florida, where she was doin' a cooking demonstration; wine connoisseurs would pair their special wines with the food she prepared. All these wine experts and vineyard owners were at the event, and neither of us being much in the drinking department, we didn't pay too much attention to anything other than the food. The event was sponsored by a mixing device company I'll call Brand A, and on the front of the stage, in three-feet-high letters, was written B R A N D A. In the foyer of the arena, they had Brand A products, especially the mixers from 1950 to the present, displayed in fancy acrylic boxes.

They introduce Paula, who walked out onstage, and the first thing she says is, "I'm not crazy about Brand A mixers."

I just about swallowed my tongue when she said that, but it was vintage Paula—no lyin' ever. The poor master of ceremonies gulped and said, "Oh, well, we would really like to thank our sponsors, Brand A." And she glared at Paula.

Here's the thing: We use Brand A products. We like them a lot. Paula likes them a lot. But when Paula was poor, she couldn't afford a serious Brand A mixer and she was usin' a cheap little hand mixer. That's what she was used to, and she especially liked usin' a glass bowl so she could see what was goin' on. The Brand A bowl was metal; it was really the bowl that bothered her. Who knew?

Somehow we got past that little stumbling block. Eventually they asked Paula if she would like to try a special wine one of the vintners was raving about.

Paula tastes it, makes a face, and says, "I really don't much like this. It tastes like baby spit-up."

No one laughs. In two sentences she has pissed off everyone in the whole place.

I give her a look and she gets what she's done. She smiles as if she's joking, and she starts drinking this wine, which really isn't so bad. But Paula's not a drinker and it don't take too much—like two glasses—before she gets a real buzz on. And in about five minutes, buzz is what she's doing.

One guy was up on the stage pushing his wine and he's saying, "This is such a fine and proud vintage and it is so smooth one can even take a bath in it; sometimes I feel like soakin' in it all day. I'm so in love with this wine."

And my Paula looks intently at this dude, and without cracking a smile says, "Well, if you did that, wouldn't it burn you down *there*?"

The guy looks at her. He didn't mean anyone to take him seriously about the takin'-a-bath part; and he really did not understand her question at all.

But I did. I knew we were headin' for trouble because after those two glasses of wine, Paula was simply a catastrophe.

The wine guy says, "I don't understand you, Miss Deen," and Paula tried to explain.

"Well, look," she tells him. "Doesn't your wine have alcohol in it? Because one time, when my momma's back was hurtin', my daddy put rubbin' alcohol on her back and it dripped down to *there* and burnt her real bad. So I don't see how you could take a bath in this wine and . . ."

If I coulda disappeared or made her disappear, I would have. From the back of the audience, I yelled out, "No more wine for Paula, *please. No more wine.*"

The audience was convulsed with laughter.

Finally, someone introduced me. I walked up to the stage, and the first thing I did was grab Paula's wineglass and move it out of her reach. She gave me that dazzlin' smile of hers, and the show went on, with Paula, thank God, being quiet for the first time in her life.

Afterward I went over to the Brand A guy and apologized. He was gracious as all get-out and said to me, "Look, as long as Paula Deen says Brand A, loud and clear, I don't care what she says about it."

What a nice company! Since then, they have been so gracious to us and we have Brand A equipment everywhere. That tells you a little about how Paula's valued as a company spokesperson, but please, if she's scheduled to appear at your function, do not refill that girl's wineglass.

My favorite meal? Well, I love a standin' rib roast and I adore potatoes. Not too slimmin'. A good steak will always get my attention but my real favorite is probably king crab legs. Paula always tells people that for me, the most romantic meal is oxtails, but that ain't true. For me, the most romantic meal is Paula cookin' any specialty she likes inside, me cookin' outside on my grill, and us meetin' together to make the meal complete. That's what I call romantic.

I already told you about Paula's inability to handle wine. Still, we both like frozen margaritas when we don't have too many challenging things to do after dinner. Every now and then I drink a glass or two of a bourbon called Blanton's, but aside from that, neither of us drinks much. I'll tell y'all how Paula discovered margaritas.

One time we went to a Chicago restaurant and the waiter says, "Could I interest y'all in a cocktail?" Well, maybe he didn't actually say *y'all.*

And Paula says, "We don't drink."

I said, "Speak for yourself. I'm full grown. Lemme order for me. I'll have a frozen margarita with salt," I told the waiter.

They brought me my drink, and before I knew what happened, Paula drank 'bout half of it and said, "Oh, Mikie, this is delicious. Just what the old pie hole needed."

Don't expect me to explain that statement. I never can explain Paula's exotic sayings.

I drank the other half and I said, "We'll have two more." So we had two more. Drank those two. Said, "We'll have two more." So we had two more. And I think we had two more. And I know that waiter had to be thinkin' after about eight of them and Paula gettin' sillier and sillier, *I would hate to see people from Georgia who do drink if these people don't drink.*

Offshore Oxtail Soup

This recipe is from my brother Father Hank Groover.
You know it's heavenly!

PREP. TIME: About 3 hours, including cooking time

SERVES: 6

2 pounds oxtails

1 medium onion

2 celery ribs

3 garlic cloves

1 small bunch parsley

1 teaspoon salt

1 bay leaf

One 29-ounce can tomato sauce

⅓ cup sugar

1⅓ cups shortening (*not* butter or margarine)

1 cup flour

1 hard-boiled egg

½ lemon, thinly sliced

1 cup dry red wine

Crusty French bread, for serving

In a deep pot, cover the oxtails with cold water and bring to a
boil over high heat. Boil for 5 minutes. Drain the oxtails, add
fresh water to cover the oxtails by at least 1 inch, and return to

the stove. Place the onion, celery, garlic, and parsley in a food processor and chop until very finely chopped; add to the soup. Add the salt and bay leaf. Cover the pot, bring to a boil, then cook at a slow simmer. When the meat is tender, after 1½ to 2 hours, turn off the heat. Add the tomato sauce.

Check to see if the soup has cooked down. If yes, add more water. In a saucepan, lightly brown the sugar in the shortening. Add the flour, stirring until absorbed in the shortening. Cook the roux until dark brown, about the color of an old penny. Slowly add the browned roux to the soup while stirring constantly. Turn the heat back on and bring to a boil. Reduce the heat so the soup simmers. The longer it simmers, at least an hour or more, the better the soup.

Before serving, add the chopped hard-boiled egg, lemon slices, and wine. Serve with crusty French bread.

The best! ⚓

8

Backstage in My Bedroom

I took my uncle to the mall the other day and we decided to grab a bite at the food court. I noticed he was watchin' a teenager sittin' right near him who had spiked hair in all different colors: red, green, orange, blue, yellow. My uncle kept starin' at him; he'd never seen anything like it. When the teenager had had enough, he asked sarcastically, "What's the matter, old man, never done anything wild in your life?"

Knowin' my uncle, and knowin' he'd have a quick response, I quickly swallowed my food so I wouldn't choke on it.

My uncle didn't bat an eye as he spoke.

"Well, I got drunk once and had sex with a peacock, and I was just wonderin' if you were my son."

I learned a lot of things courtesy of my wife Paula Deen, and I've had a lot of wild adventures, but none so fun as those things I've learned and experienced because of her, in my own home, in my own bedroom—but also in my livin' room and kitchen and wherever else you'd think a cast of hundreds would want to go in the house on Turner's Creek.

Why a cast of hundreds? Well, there's Paula and me and the dogs of course, and the kin family when they're over here. Our extended work family is usually around: Barry Weiner, Theresa Feuger, Brandon Branch, Nancy Assuncao, Michelle White, Hollis Johnson, Jamie Cribbs, Courtney Fix, Sarah Meighan, and Patrick Dobbs, not to mention the entire cast of *Paula's Best Dishes,* which is filmed right here in our very own kitchen. From all of them, I've learned not only how to live in ways I'd never dream, but also how to change my life in ways I never considered. Some people I avoided because they were so different from me, I don't avoid anymore. Some things I didn't understand, I now understand.

All will be clear before you get to the end of this chapter.

First of all, just imagine what it's like to have people walking in on you in the bedroom or bathroom even though those people feel like family. Well, it's sure never a dull moment. I can't recall anybody walkin' in while I was naked (not that I would be embarrassed). But I really try not to be buck naked during a filming. It's kinda like knowin' your sister's wanderin' around the house. Thirty sisters wanderin' around.

What are they all doing here? Well, even though it creates some problems, it was the lesser of several evils to film right here in our home.

First of all, you've got to know that it takes about two weeks to film the season's worth of nine to eleven of *Paula's Best Dishes* episodes. When Paula started filming her television show eight years ago, she had to fly to Millbrook, New York, which is where her executive producer, Gordon Elliott, lives. We'd decided to film from his home rather than a studio because it was very picturesque—cute dog, beautiful house, country kitchen, pretty countryside—you git it. But after we were done filming for the day, then what? I mean, we didn't live there, our family wasn't there, and in two days frankly you could see everything there is to see in Millbrook. Also, after a while, flying to New York, then making a two-hour ride to get to Millbrook so often was a lotta wear 'n' tear on all of us, but we could see it was really gettin' to Paula.

It finally came to a head when once, on a weekend off, we stayed at a fabulous bed-and-breakfast in Millbrook. I'd said to the proprietor, "Lord, this is a great old place! What did it used to be?"

She answered, "At one time it was a theater, but before that, it was a recruitin' center for the Union army."

"I don't know if I can stay here tonight," I told Paula later, "with all those damn Yankee scallywags ghostin' around."

Well, I made it through the night, but we began to think about filmin' closer to home. In Savannah, we were just in the process of building our new home. Why not film *Paula's Best Dishes* right there in our present home? I think it's way more picturesque than Millbrook, New York, and in the background our viewers might be lucky enough to see a dolphin or two jumping; our kitchen is large and comfy, we have a big ol' deep fryer set into the counter, we have our painting of the big ol' rooster on the wall, and Paula's grandson, Jack, might wander in with his momma and daddy.

And yes, it is a lot less wear 'n' tear on Paula. Now, in between scenes or when people are settin' up (which takes interminable amounts of time) she can go take a nap in her own bed, use her own bathroom, watch her own TV, talk to Jamie and Bobby or Brooke or Corrie on her own phone.

So when thirty people minimum descend on us and my bedroom becomes part of backstage with four people working at the same time with Paula on hair, makeup, and clothing—not even paying attention to the bearded lump in the bed—I remind myself that it's a trade-off from filming far away from home. It also showcases Savannah, the city we love, and encourages tourism here, which the public officials like a lot. This is what I wanted, and that's what we accomplished.

Most folk, if they had this many people wanderin' through their house, would be worried about their valuables. But with us, everyone is trusted. These young people are just as honest as they can be and we trust 'em with everything. It's a Southern thing. They can go into my office and use my computer, go into our refrigerator to see what was left over from last night, go into the bathroom in search of a Band-Aid; every part of the house is open to them. Frankly, I love these people to death, I'm glad to see 'em arrive—but then, I'm very, very, very glad to see 'em leave.

My home resembles a wild country fair during a shoot. On a wall in the kitchen—which is actually the set for the show—is the rooster picture that all America is so familiar with now. But frankly, if I wanted to walk into my kitchen and pour myself a cuppa coffee, I'd be walkin' through the set while the cameras are rollin'. So, I wait for my coffee breaks.

Each person has a specific and very important job and all kinds of things go on backstage. The crew is very friendly. Everybody likes each other. It's like the operating room before surgery. If you walked onto the set, this is what you'd see: Brandon Branch, Paula's main man, would be running around checking the placement of the flowers he's actually grown in our backyard. Well, actually, Brandon's the flower stylist and he's appointed himself the prop stylist, the wardrobe stylist, the food stylist—the *everything* stylist, including the Paula stylist. His job is to make sure everything looks beautiful at all times, including her and her surroundings, even though there is an official hairstylist, makeup stylist, food stylist, and prop person. There are script people checking scripts, others welcoming guests, others making sure the food for the show is fresh and camera-ready, others vacuuming the set, others checking sound levels, others taking camera shots . . . well, you get it.

I've had to get used to living with this spectacle. What the television viewer doesn't see when he or she watches Paula's programs are all the people who have been marching in and out of my home, making all look beautiful for the shoot. You'd think from watching *Paula's Best Dishes* there was never a dirty dish sittin' on the counter or a Paula with her hair in fat rollers emerging, sleepy-eyed, from a ten-minute afternoon nap. There's Brandon again, fooling now with some green apples somewhere: Looks like he might take a chunk out o' one, but no, he's figuring out where and in what arrangement they'll look best.

It all looks like chaos, but it's not. Well, it's controlled chaos, I guess. I mean, when you've got seven dogs, twenty members of Paula's family just hangin' out in the livin' room, agents, lawyers, restaurant managers who have dropped in for a hello with the boss, advertising agencies, Web people, writers to fix any holes in the script, food stylists to make what seems to have just come out of the oven look delectable, the catering woman who is already setting up lunch out on the patio for the cast of hundreds all coming and going, backstage in my bedroom, maybe when I'm wanting to pull on a pair of shorts, I got to be pretty cool. I know no one cares about my shorts, all they want and need to do is make Paula and the house gorgeous for a fabulous show.

Does it work? Sure does. It's *why* the show works, maintains Gordon Elliott, precisely because this is the place the star lives. What matters, he says, is that Paula feels comfortable, and that's why you get the show that millions of people tune in to, to see their best friend.

What makes Paula most comfortable is her family poppin' in to be on the show or even her oldest friends makin' an unexpected appearance. Last week, Bubbles (aka Susan Green) from Albany, Georgia, where Paula grew up, was on her show. Paula was frying cupcakes and she asked Bubbles to set them in the oven. Well, who knew it, but Bubbles was wearing her tap shoes from when she and Paula were girls, and she had her bubble wand with her as well.

"I never travel without my taps in the trunk of the car," Bubbles announced. Why the hell she carries those taps around, I don't know, but she was pretty cute as, blowin' her trademark bubbles all the way, she tap-tapped those cupcakes clear across the set and into the oven. Gordon never stopped the cameras for a moment.

"That's what makes this show unique," he said. "Nowhere else on the Food Network shows will you have a blond, tap-dancing best friend doing 360s all the way to the oven, giving you beat to the beats. It's just so great. And when someone watches the show," Gordon predicted, "guarantee she will say to her friend the next day, 'Did you see that hilarious woman blowin' bubbles and tap-dancing her cupcakes into the oven on Paula Deen's show?' Better press you cannot get."

Bubbles is known for her pithy comments, like "You have to air your wares," and by that she means if you don't tell it all, somebody else is goin' to tell it or show it for you. Paula airs her wares a whole lot.

To me it feels like real life, the way we squeeze out a television show. One good part is that Paula's here, not travelin', and I love that, especially when I'm takin' a break from my own work. When she leaves the set for twenty minutes while they're doing their prep work, Paula will go in our bedroom, sit down, and watch Nancy Grace on TV. She picks up her Diet Coke, sits up there with her dogs and me, and when Gordon's ready, he calls her and she goes back on the set, all relaxed and happy.

Sometimes I can't figure out who's sittin' in my livin' room, and that's because they're often perfect strangers. A week ago, I came home and all of the usual culprits were runnin' around doin' their jobs. Gordon was sittin' up in his big director chair so I knew all was right with the world—but who on earth were those two pretty blondes sittin' there laughin', gettin' the biggest kick out of the proceedin's?

So I asked them. "Who are you?"

Turns out they were two sisters from Philadelphia. They'd bid a whole lot of money for a day behind the scenes at a Paula Deen show for an Arthur Ashe Youth Tennis and Education Association auction and fund-raiser in their city. Damned if they didn't win and there they were, sittin' in my house, observin', laughin,' and chattin' for all the world like they lived there. You just never know. They also won a dinner at The Lady & Sons restaurant, and boy, will they have tales to tell when they get home.

Sometimes things go wrong.

One day, around eight in the mornin', I heard the most blood-curdling yell comin' from the porch off the kitchen. I ran downstairs and found forty or so otherwise efficient people frozen in horror—all these smart-ass television people were standin' there, paralyzed with fear. Seems a water rat from the creek outside had lost his direction and found his way to the house. There he was, sittin' as cool as you please, right on top of the outside swing. "It's a rat, a *raaaaat,*" screamed the prop gal.

I jumped out of bed thinking it's just Paula playin' around with the rubber toy she sometimes terrorizes staff with, but no, it was a real, big, ugly ol' black water rat, 'bout a foot long countin' tail. Everyone, frozen in place, was just looking at him and screamin'. Actually, Paula really does have a black rubber rat she fools around with; she often throws it into the middle of polite company every now and then to scare the pants off them and maybe make them less boring. So the staff all thought that's what it was at first, but when the "rubber" rat moved, all bets were off.

So I ran downstairs thinking someone was getting killed, saw this thing, got the fire poker, and shooed him off the swing back to his rightful home, the creek. Then they had to disinfect the entire show set even if he touched nothin'—every pan, every fork—just in case the rat had passed by the kitchen on its way to the porch swing. Other things happen in the middle of a show to convince everyone if they weren't already convinced that this is a home, not a cold television set.

For example, we'll be in the middle of a show and someone will telephone the house. If she feels like it, Paula will take that call in the middle of the show. Usually the cameras keep rolling; they never know what good material will come from that call. Then Paula will very politely explain to the person that Miss Deen isn't available right now, but you know, if the caller wants to come around and drop off, you know, Michael's repaired Jet Ski, it would be fine. And she'll spend five minutes on the phone explaining to this guy *where* he should drop off my Jet Ski. That's Paula. Someone else would pick up the phone and say, "What the hell are you doing? I'm in the middle of a TV show. You gotta hang up, hang up fast! "

But my wife never loses her cool.

Paula's macaw is the biggest problem for the director. Ladybird lives in a giant cage on the porch off the kitchen. She's a giant blue and gold macaw and she's been with Paula through all the bad times. Sometimes when Paula had nothing to eat, she'd find a way to feed Ladybird. She would even sleep with Paula, and as a result this bird thinks Paula is its momma. Ladybird calls for momma, loud and clear—"Momma, Momma"—at 4:00 PM on the button, right in the middle of the filmin'. Go explain that to millions of viewers. It drives our executive producer, Gordon, absolutely nuts. He says he's done a whole mess of TV shows in his time, but he never had to stop shootin' for a damn parrot.

Paula wouldn't hear of banishing Ladybird to some other part of the house, so we figured out something pretty ingenious if I do say so myself. We had a photograph of Paula, laughing and looking very natural, made into a life-size cardboard statue. One day we put the statue right in front of Ladybird's cage when she was yellin' momma and . . . silence. The bird felt totally comforted with her "Momma" standin' there. Doesn't say much for bird intelligence or for their sense of smell, but it worked for us. Now we set that statue out in front of Ladybird's cage every day before filmin' starts.

Sometimes what goes wrong is caused by Paula's wicked sense of humor. Along with the rubber rat, I'm sorry to tell y'all, she has her own little fart machine.

One day, the cast was all here filmin', and I was watchin' from the sidelines. Paula was makin' a broccoli recipe, and in the middle of the recipe, she's sitting up there on her chair and says, "Oh, hey, y'all, I don't know, but that broccoli's not sittin' too well in my stomach." All of a sudden we hear this, like, *Bbllllpppppp*. And we're all, like, oh, God, she pooped her pants or somethin'. Stop the cameras! When she did it again, I went over to her and said, "Paula, is everything okay?"

Well, she was just laughin' to beat the band, and she takes out this fart machine, and plays it long and steady for everybody assembled. Dignity is not a requisite for participation on the Paula Deen show, at least backstage in my bedroom.

Sometimes it takes very little to screw up when your home is a TV set. I can come home from work starving, walk into my kitchen in between shoots, and see a terrific loaf of bread or a roll. It looks so good so I pick it up and I'm dying to set my teeth right into it. Then someone says, 'Whoops! Don't eat that, Michael. It's for the show."

Now how am I supposed to know that? This is my kitchen, the hot oil fryer is my hot oil fryer, and the balsamic vinegar is what Paula will use to make us dinner later on. The bin in which they store tomatoes and peppers for the set? Those tomatoes and peppers will be used for my dinner tonight.

Couldn't that roll be sitting there ready for me to chomp into?

Nope, it may be my kitchen, but it's Paula's show.

It's true that you really have to watch the watchers when you're doing a food show. You never know who will eat up the scenery.

On some cooking shows, the food might be sprayed with an inedible product to make it look better. On Paula's show, food is never sprayed with anything, so it has a way of disappearing. Right before the election, Paula had Michelle Obama as her guest and they cooked some yummy fried shrimp. Well, all of us watching the taping were drooling while Paula and Mrs. Obama were up there gettin' their fill of those delectable shrimp during the whole show.

When the filmin' was finally complete, Libby, Paula's food stylist, walked from the kitchen carrying a beautiful platter of fresh fried shrimp. Seeing the tray, Mrs. Obama says, "Well, I'll have just one more."

With that, I asked Libby if I could have 'em.

She says, "Yes, you can have 'em."

So when she says you can have 'em, I think that's what she means, that you can have 'em—all of 'em.

But what Libby meant is I could have *one*. And then she walked away to talk with Mrs. Obama.

So, I said, "Courtney, try these shrimp. Jamie, try these shrimp.

Brandon, try these. Gordon, try these." There we were, eatin' 'em all up, and when she came back, Libby 'bout blew a fuse. She was wanting to take a picture of those shrimp that could be used when the credits were rollin'. She *meant*, she carefully explained, I could have *one* shrimp—and now she had to fry up a whole new batch. *Next time, be specific, girl,* I thought to myself.

I've explained why I have to fight to get into my own bathroom when a show's being filmed. Sometimes I can't ever get in, even if I put up the good fight. This morning started out pretty good when two members of the cast brought us coffee to wake us up, which it did. Then Paula takes a shower. Then she needs her makeup and hair done. I realize I ain't never goin' to get in that bathroom till five o'clock this afternoon. So instead o' me waitin' or takin' a shower when everybody's occupyin' the bathroom, I just got into my car and drove out to the Garaj Mahal (as I call my new state-of-the-art garage!) in the new house we're buildin' down the road, and took a shower and came back. It was a long way to go for a shower.

Now, I'd like to talk about something else that's hard for me to discuss. I'm a private man; I don't wear my heart on my sleeve and if something embarrasses me, some action I've taken or not taken, some stupid opinions I've let be known, I sure don't discuss it with the world. The good and the bad things about me usually stay behind the scenes where nobody knows about them but me. And maybe Paula.

I better start writing faster before I change my mind about revealing so much of myself in this book. Some of the things I'm about to say are not pretty.

You gotta remember that I'm a river man. River men drink and curse and chase women. We talk like a bunch of sailors, which we are. Most of us have good hearts but we're simply not exposed to certain kinds of people—and when we are, we freeze. We get, well, nervous.

Without insultin' too many people, I think I can safely say that I and the guys I hung out with before I met Paula were homophobes. I am sorry to admit that. We did not understand gay people. We couldn't figure out what they *did*, and we'd hurt anyone who even thought about doin' it to us. I mean that. Mostly we thought guys who were light in the loafers humped your leg like a dog would.

Then I met Paula, who had lots of different kinds of people in her world. Some of them—many of them—were out-and-out gay. And I mean *out*.

In particular, Paula's number one right-hand man, now and forever, is Brandon Branch. I think it would not be an exaggeration to say that in the beginning, I was very uncomfortable with him because Brandon is very gay. I was also wary of her show hairdresser, Jamie Cribbs, for the same reason. I would have knocked your block off if you accused me of being scared of these guys back then; I would have said I didn't like them, or that they were queer, or that I didn't care to know anything about them—woulda said anything but the truth, which was that I didn't *get* them. I'd never had a gay friend or a gay colleague. Just didn't know how to talk to them.

I wasn't the only one. Hollis Johnson, my friend who acts as Paula's bodyguard or, as he would put it, Paula's fourth son, was also homophobic.

Now, when you spend time, day after day, year after year, with a person, you get to know them. You get to be easy with them and their humor, which in Brandon's case is pretty sharp. For so long, it was me, Brandon, and Paula—a trio. And little by little, I am happy to tell you, my attitudes changed. Paula was at the bottom of it, of course. She owns restaurants where some of the waiters are gay, and a lot of people in the television and film industry are gay. So I've not only met really great and interesting gay men now, but talked with them for long hours, gone drinkin' with them, grown to appreciate them, and with two in particular, come to love them as sons. That would be Brandon Branch and Jamie Cribbs.

Brandon says I'm coming to be more in touch with my feminine side. I will not put that in bold letters in this book, but maybe it's true.

But how my world has changed! It's been said that Southerners are prejudiced and racially biased, whatever that means. Well, when the people closest to Paula and me travel together as a crew on the road, as we always do, we're quite a sight. Our team includes two gay men, one black man, a Chinese-Jewish agent, two Yankee women, and a redneck couple—that would be Paula and me. It doesn't get any better than that. We have some fine old times.

What I learned from Paula? To see people clearly as they really are.

My friend Hollis and I were the worst. And last week, Brandon was walkin' around telling everyone he'd seen both of us in a gay bar in Key West.

It was true! We were there because Paula had an appearance to make in Florida. Brandon was walkin' down the street, peeked into a gay bar, and there was Hollis and me. We'd rented motorcycles, and as we were toolin' around, we saw Paula's wonderful and fun hairdresser Jamie and his partner Jay in this gay bar. So we went in to have a beer with them.

I don't have to say that would never have happened six years ago. But when people practically live with you as they do during the filming sessions backstage in my bedroom, you get to know them. And honor them. And in some cases, love them.

Furthermore, if anyone ever messed with Brandon or his partner,

Jim, or Jamie or Jay when I was around, it would be just like some-one was messin' with my brother or sister.

Brandon tells me that he feels closer to me than anyone else on this planet now.

That means more to me than I can ever tell you.

Brandon also says he thinks I'm turnin' gay. I may kill him.

Bluewater Braised Red Cabbage in Apple Cider

Braising red (or green) cabbage with fresh fruit is very common in the German community. The Groovers of Georgia trace their roots in this country back to 1734 and the Saltzburger settlement of Ebenezer on the Savannah River. Though often thought of as a holiday dish, this is a delicious accompaniment to any pork or wild game dish.

PREP TIME: 1 hour, including cooking time

SERVES: 6 to 8

¼ cup butter

1 cup sliced onions

¼ cup diced celery

1 teaspoon diced garlic

3 pounds or 15 cups shredded red cabbage

1 cup apple juice

2 cups grated peeled apples

½ cup chicken stock

1 tablespoon sugar

2 bay leaves

Salt and fresh cracked black pepper to taste

In a cast-iron pot, melt the butter over medium-high heat. Sauté the onions, celery, and garlic 3 to 5 minutes, or until the vegetables are wilted. Stir in the shredded cabbage and cook 30 minutes, stirring occasionally, until the cabbage begins to wilt. Blend in the apple juice, apples, chicken stock, and sugar. Add the bay leaves and continue cooking, uncovered, 15 to 20 minutes. Season with salt and pepper. Remove the bay leaves and serve. ⚓

9

Romance with Paula

This man was marrying his sweetheart of four years. There was one fly in the ointment: Her younger sister was just gorgeous and she flirted like hell with her future brother-in-law.

One day she says, "I just picked up your weddin' invitations. Come on over to my house and look at 'em."

When he got there, she says, "You know I would like to have one fling with you before you commit your life with my sister.'

The guy was stunned. He didn't know what to say.

"I'm goin' upstairs," she says, "and if you'd like to have one wild time before you get married, come on up there."

Well, that guy ran like crazy to his car.

And as he did, he saw his whole future family was right outside the younger sister's house, standin' near his car. His future father-in-law came over to him and said, "Welcome to the family, son. You're exactly what we prayed for, someone we could trust our daughter with."

Moral of the story: Always keep your condoms in the car.

Kiddin', just kiddin'.

Listen: I'm a guy with a capital G. This is a hard chapter to write. Guys, especially tugboat pilots, don't talk excessively about romance, if you know what I mean. Makes me damn uncomfortable. So, I'm goin' to share the writin' of this part of my book with Paula, who doesn't have a whole lot of trouble talkin' about anything.

I have to start by sayin' one thing: Paula gives me unwaverin' unconditional support. Nothing ever changes in her deepest heart; she's always the same there. No matter whether she likes me at the moment or not, she always loves me. I never saw that in any woman before. That's what I call romantic.

You know, I once heard some people sayin' they thought Paula and I just had a business relationship. That really made me laugh. Paula is the only brilliant businessperson in this twosome, not me, and she would have come out on the short end of the stick of this marriage if she married me only for my business acumen, or for what she could get from me that would enhance her business. Maybe there are some small things I teach her about human character that translates into business, but believe me, she'd be just where she is today if her dogs had never gone poopin' in my backyard. And I'd probably be exactly where I was then, but a whole lot lonelier.

Maybe the best way I can express it is that my life with Paula is complete in the sharing of everything, as great in the bedroom as it is in the kitchen, and business hasn't got two cents to do with the romance part. That's sayin' somethin'. We've not talked about our romantic moments much, until now, that is. But so many people ask Paula and me separately just what makes us so happy, so *affectionate*, at this stage of our lives. I think what we have found is so great it should be bottled and so I've decided to talk a little bit about the nature of our love in this chapter. Paula can fill in with the rest—I just can't write some things down.

One day not too long ago Paula was on the *Today* show and I was sittin' in the audience. Someone from the stage asked me which is better, her cookin' or her lovin.' Imagine asking that on national television?

I think I blew that questioner out of the water with my answer, if I do say so myself. I said, "Paula feeds both my heart and my stomach. No, she *fills* my heart and my stomach." Pretty smooth, no?

We are best friends. We are best sexual as well as affectionate partners; we can't keep our hands off each other.

Paula loves to relax in our big, comfortable bed. In some ways, it's really the center of the house and our life. She watches television from there; she talks with family, friends, and business associates on the telephone from bed; and she even worked on practically her whole memoir from that bed. Friends, family, reporters, music listeners, television watchers, my kids, her kids, seven dogs—everyone ends up piling onto the bed with Paula. That's just the way she is— comfy and welcoming.

But eventually, everyone 'cept the dogs goes home. The bed changes into something else entirely. It becomes the center of our romantic relationship. I'm not talkin' just about sex but about huggin' and listenin' and sharin' and even sometimes cryin'. It's only *our* place then. No one else is invited.

We do admire each other somethin' fierce.

There you go.

The *Paula and Michael Show*, comin' up.

Paula: We're just different when it comes to expressin' romance. It's me who kisses and hugs and handholds. On our anniversary, it's me who goes over with the first kiss. I'm a toucher, no doubt about it.

Michael: I'm the touchee.

Paula: My number one need in this relationship—that Jimmy Deen and I both somehow neglected in my first marriage—is loyalty, absolute loyalty where I know I can say anything to Michael and it won't be repeated anywhere. The loyalty that comes from knowin' that the other is unfailingly true, no matter what it looks like on television or anywhere else. The loyalty that means I always know where he is every minute. Well, approximately every minute. I'd call that unconditional love. I just love this man, no matter where he is, what he says.

Michael: Same answer. I never lived with that kind of loyalty before. When we're apart, we check in with each other constantly. More than constantly. I trust her with my life, even though I don't trust that what she says next won't embarrass me somethin' awful.

Let me give you an example: When we were first datin' we were invited to a pretty fancy party. The woman who held the party introduced her boyfriend as her "significant other." And Paula, out of the clear blue sky, said, "I hate that phrase—significant other."

"Well, what do you call Michael?" the woman asked.

And Paula said, "Well, I sure don't call him my boyfriend either, because he's not a boy. I call him my man."

And that woman asked Paula, kind of snooty, "What does Michael call *you*?"

Paula had had enough and with a twinkle in her eye that only I recognized, she up and said real polite, "He calls me his bitch. But he says it so *romantically.*"

And oh, I about died. If I coulda disappeared, I woulda.

Paula: When Michael and I first met, I couldn't caress him enough. And I think at one point he almost got tired of it. I was all over him, I wouldn't leave him alone. I kinda have to keep that in check. I need the touchin', the foreplay I guess people call it, more than he. Michael is not as playful as I am and I have to respect that. People are different in their emotional needs. I can't get enough touching. Michael can.

You know, when I haven't seen him for a while and he walks into the room—say, if I'm on the set—and I look up and see Michael, well, I can't help it, my stomach does a little flip. That's just the way I am. You know, when you're younger and you start out in a relationship, it goes through different stages. You can't stay eighteen and at the peak of your libido. But I still feel that excitement and that tingle. And sometimes, when I just *think* about things we've done, there goes my stomach again, doin' that flip.

Michael: I get that stomach flip, too. I love Paula and I want to be with her from sunrise to sunset. I think I tell her that or at least *mean* to tell her that in a million different ways, maybe not so much in words.

Paula: Hold on, there: There's some things people think the other is just 'sposed to know. Well, some of us forget and we need to be retold the things. I'll need to hear that you love me again and again. I'll need it about 473 times more this year. You need to say the words, big boy.

Michael: Another thing: I think romance lives along with independence. People need to have some room to make their own mistakes and decisions, then come back to the other for a hug, even if they've made a whopper of a mistake.

Paula: Oh, yes. You have to stay true to yourself even if it's not the decision your spouse would make.

Michael: You know, some people are constantly judging each other. Badly. I try to support and compliment Paula on most everything she does.

Paula: That's true. Undying support he gives me, no matter what. If he saw me eat a whole chocolate cake, he'd say, "Slide over and I'll help y'all with that." Sometimes, when we're both in the mood for lovemaking, I'll get all tickled and indulge in some horseplay, and Michael, even though he's dying for the main act, plays along. Too much, he gets real aggravated with my jokiness. He's very sensitive, you know. I have to try to be more aware of his sensitivities.

Look, I'm sensitive about a lot of things, too. For example, I don't know if I ever told you this, Michael, but I feel shy when it's time to take off my clothes. Did you know that?

Michael: No.

Paula: Well, do you know this? In other romantic relationships, I always liked a lot of people around—not for the lovemaking, of course, but for the prelude to the lovemakin': the parties, the eatin' dinner, that stuff. But I'm happy as a pig in sunshine to have just me and you alone most of the time. Did you know that?

Michael: Oh, yeah, I feel the same way. You know, I'm writing this on our fifth anniversary, with you sittin' right beside me. This morning you came into the livin' room. It was swarmin' with people and seven dogs runnin' and food all over the place because of the shoot today. You ignored everyone and everything else, and you came right over to me and looked deep at me with those gorgeous eyes, and you held my face with both hands and said, "Ain't life good, Michael?" Well, it is, and the way you said that promised so many other things in our private life that I can't wait till everyone goes home. If that isn't romantic—without spellin' out everything else, which I don't intend to—I don't know what is.

You know, Paula's life exposes us to so many people that it's a real bonus to get away sometimes and be just the two of us. It's rare, but it happens, and when it does, then *I'm* as happy as a pig in sunshine also. But I'll say this: Paula has a knack, even if there are a million folks around, of making me feel it's just her and me in the room. What's that worth?

You know when everyone's young and they look at people fifty or sixty, they think we're ready to go out to pasture. But I'm here to tell you it's not so. Boy, is it not so with Paula! She is one sexy lady. I'm lookin' forward to eighty and, Lord willin', ninety. Look: That's all you're going to get from me about our sex life in this chapter. I've heard that women go into women's locker rooms and they just talk, talk about the most personal stuff. Well, I don't know that it's so, but I never met a man who told other people about such details.

Paula: Men are worse. I never met a man who didn't tell the same story: If I listened I'd *believe* that each one is hung like a mule and can go for hours. But its funny, I have never yet met that man who's hung like a mule and can last past fifteen minutes. Except for you, Michael.

Michael: Oh, my, I think having invited my wife into the writin' of this chapter made it certain I'm going to hate this chapter. Sometimes when she comes out with personal stuff like that I can understand why people drink. Let me say this about what she just said: The good Lord has a way of working things out. As our bodies change and deteriorate, so do our eyes so we both look perfect to each other. 'Cause we can't see.

I could have a lot more to say in this chapter, you know, but I don't want to. Why? Because I don't want our children rippin' out this page.

Gettin' back to keeping passion in a marriage, I think it helps when two people surprise each other occasionally. It's been my experience with Paula.

By surprise I mean like givin' presents without rhyme or reason. For example, as I write, Paula is wearing diamond earrings I bought her without it bein' any special occasion. I just brought 'em home one day and got amply rewarded, which I shouldn't have even said.

Paula: Michael really has an eye for jewelry and I wouldn't dream of buying anything without him lookin' at it first. He often surprises me with little things like that. I wish I could say I do the same for him, but I don't. Not that I don't buy him gifts—just look at that fancy car sittin' out there in the Garaj Mahal—but I knew he wanted it and it was for his birthday, so it was no surprise. I'm gonna start surprising him more, now that I think about it. And I know just how I'll start.

I want to say something: I once read that what a man or woman does for a livin' isn't just what they do for a livin': What they do for that livin' is actually what they are as a man or woman. You are what you do! I think romance comes when the other respects what you are. I know Michael respects my work because it's what I am, else he couldn't go along with me in practically every aspect of it.

Michael: Oh, without a doubt, I do. It's opened up worlds to me. And I know Paula respects what I do for a livin'. I feel blessed to be able to go on these big ships. I get to see the sunrise and whales at play and I get to work with my son and son-in-law and many of my friends, who are career river men doing the same kind of work like I have for thirty or forty years.

Paula: I surely do respect that. It's one of the things that attracted me to Michael at first because it's a very sexy job. A very, very sexy job.

Michael: You know why they call a boat "her"? It's because she's unpredictable.

Paula: Oh, so sexy. He's in charge of this thousand-ton vehicle and he makes her do what she has to do, what she was born to do. If that's not sexy, I don't know what is.

Michael: You know, I'm interested that Paula says and believes that. I used to think that my way with boats, when I came to this marriage, was sorta intimidatin'; it was a kind of baggage I brought with me. In my line of work, I give commands, I give orders, there's no time for negotiatin.' I don't ask for opinions or take votes. When you bring that along with you, it's not real good for a marriage.

Paula: But then, when you marry a woman who's as strong as you are in many ways—well, don't you see how a man who can make a powerful boat do what she was born to do can also make a powerful woman do what she was born to do? Whew—I find that very sensual and romantic. I've always been so proud to tell people what Michael does for a livin' and how passionately he feels about his work.

Michael: Same here. I can't talk enough about how I feel about Paula's accomplishments and the accolades she receives. It's a romantic turn-on to go home with a person you respect so totally. It's . . . well, *she* came home with *me*. Think about it!

Paula: There's somethin' I want to say here. When I was young, I always thought the most sexy, romantic guy was the guy who was stacked with muscles and brawn and youth. Well, now, Michael's got the muscles and brawn but he, like me, doesn't really have the youth anymore. And you know what? It does not turn me off one bit, not one bit, not even one drop. Frankly? It makes things better.

Michael: I don't want to talk about that.

Paula: Too bad, I'm talking. I guess if I was eighteen years old and I had seen someone, a mature man who looked like Michael, to think I could have been attracted to him—well, that would sound totally insane then. But Michael's right: I guess God does something to us inside, some kind of magic he puts in us, in me especially, so that as I mature, I find that little belly on Michael very, very attractive. *Yummy*. I think women anyway are much more forgiving about imperfections than men.

Michael: Oh, God.

Paula: Do the signs of aging in me turn you off, Michael?

Michael: No, you're perfect. Do we have to talk about this anymore?

Paula: Yes. I love to taste Michael. *Mmmmmmm*.

Michael: Oh, God. Turn off that tape recorder.

Paula: You know what? I'm so aware of his feelings, that affects me in every way, not just sexually. When things are great between us, I feel wittier, more playful, more desirable, more adorable. And if we were havin' a little tiff, you know what? I couldn't go onstage. I could not do it. I would have to make sure that what was wrong between us was fixed. I would have to resolve it. When it comes to Michael, I just can't blow off hard feelings between us. And you know what? I think there's something awful romantic in that.

Michael: I'm probably better than Paula at hidin' things and blockin' them out. So could I go do my work if Paula and I had a little fight in the mornin'? Probably yes. But it's rare I have bad feelings about Paula, and if I ever do, I get over them damn fast. Somehow, she makes it so neither of us can hold a grudge. How great is that?

This last part of the chapter is for Paula's eyes. Oh, hell—y'all can read it too, but since I'm not so good with the talkin' about romance, I write this only to you, Paula Deen.

You alone.

I'll never forget: Someone once asked me what I'd say to Paula if somehow I knew she only had fifteen minutes to live. All I had was fifteen minutes to say my last words to her. I've thought about it. This is what I say to you, darlin':

You mean everything to me. We met at a time when I thought I would be by myself for the rest of my life, and I was okay with that. I'm a tough guy, I can do anything, I can even live with loneliness. Until I met you. You know, you taught me how to live and how to love. And, you know, I feel that if you only have fifteen minutes to live, this is the end of my life too; in a very real way, it surely is. If you are to die, I don't know how I'll pick up the pieces and go on. Please leave the back door of heaven cracked if I don't make it through the front pearly gates.

I loved the time we had together. No man ever loved a woman more. I love you more than ice cream.

Shoreside Shrimp Salad

This is also great on a sandwich!

PREP TIME: 20 to 30 minutes

SERVES: 2 to 4

1 hard-boiled egg
2 cups cooked shrimp, chopped and chilled
1 cup finely chopped celery
1 tablespoon finely minced onion
1 tablespoon fresh lemon juice
½ cup mayonnaise
Salt and pepper to taste
Romaine lettuce or mixed greens
Thinly sliced tomatoes
Avocado slices, optional
Tomato wedges, optional

In a medium bowl, mash the hard-boiled egg with a fork. Mix in the shrimp with the celery, onion, lemon juice, mayonnaise, and salt and pepper to taste. Serve on a bed of romaine lettuce or mixed greens and sliced tomatoes. Garnish with avocado slices or tomato wedges, if desired. ⚓

10

Gettin' Rid of the Dry Rot

A man boarded an airplane and took his seat. As he settled in, he glanced up and saw the most beautiful woman boarding the plane. He soon realized she was heading straight toward him. As fate would have it, she took the seat right beside his.

Eager to strike up a conversation, he blurted out, "Business trip or pleasure?"

She turned, smiled, and said, "Business. I'm going to the Annual Nymphomaniacs of America Convention in Boston."

He swallowed hard. Here was the most gorgeous woman he had ever seen sitting next to him, and she was going to a meeting of nymphomaniacs.

Struggling to maintain his composure, he calmly asked, "What's your business role at this convention?"

"Lecturer," she responded. "I use information that I have learned from my personal experiences to debunk some of the popular myths about sexuality."

"Really?" he said. "And what kind of myths are there?"

"Well," she explained, "one popular myth is that African-

American men are the most well endowed of all men, when in fact it is the Native American Indian who is most likely to possess that trait. Another popular myth is that Frenchmen are the best lovers, when actually it is men of Jewish descent who are the best. I have also discovered that the lover with absolutely the best stamina is the Southern redneck."

Suddenly the woman became a little uncomfortable and blushed.

"I'm sorry," she said, "I shouldn't really be discussing all of this with you. I don't even know your name."

"Tonto," the man said. "Tonto Goldstein, but my friends call me Bubba."

It's no myth that a wooden boat's a livin' thing, and it must be used in the water or else it gets dry rot, a disease that decays the timber so it becomes brittle and rotten. Water is the boat's medium, the thing that keeps it alive; it's like air for humans. Without water and with nonuse, dry rot starts in the guts of the boat and it isn't even visible to folks until the boat literally starts to fall apart.

Dry rot can cause instability and collapse in other kinds of powerful structures—a great marriage, say. Paula and I are determined to keep dry rot out of our marriage at any cost. Dry rot creeps in silently and unexpectedly and sometimes in the most innocent ways.

The medium for marriage is communication, trust, and respect. When you neglect a marriage and don't use it, don't feed it, when you don't talk to your partner, don't share affection and surprises and humor and adventures, a marriage gets dry rot. Even a good marriage can get eaten away from the inside and start to decay from poor communication.

Lack of trust is a dry rot producer. How can you be with someone you don't really trust? I trust Paula in all things. However, if I don't preface a secret I'm tellin' her by saying something like, "This is not for national TV or even for Brandon or Bubbles; it's just between us," chances are I'll hear my secret shared with the universe on Paula's TV show or on Rachael Ray. It's hard for her to hide her thoughts—that's how honest and real she is. If I tell her somethin' privately, she has difficulty seeing why she can't tell it to her pals, who, as far as she's concerned, number in the millions. She's getting better about it, she really is, especially when I take the time to say, "Paula, this is just between us two." Without a doubt, couples have to keep the other's trust—and if one makes a mistake, he or she better know how to say they're sorry, something that's not as easy as breathin' for me.

Criticism is another issue that can cause dry rot. Most of the time the criticism I get from Paula is meant lovingly and in such good faith, but it still hurts. I think couples have to be real careful about the way they tell their mates they don't look just right or sound just right to the partner's liking. Let me give you an example.

I'm a very hairy person. I guess Paula has gotten tired of telling me to groom some errant hairs, so she's gotten to be compulsive about constantly pluckin' hairs out of me. Whether I'm drivin', readin', or sleepin', it really doesn't matter—here comes Paula with her fingernails to pluck out any stray hair that's sprouting from my nose or ears. I probably got more hair on my ears than the dogs, and as far as Paula's concerned, it's got to be removed immediately. So I'll give her five minutes to do her preenin' and after the five minutes, I'm finished. I got so much hair in my beard and mustache, no one's gonna pick up that one hair peeking out from my nose; that's what I believe. Paula's different. She thinks she can make me pretty. Too late.

Well, I'll let her tell it.

Paula: Lemme tell ya, I did get real bad about preenin' Michael. When you get to be a certain age, somehow that hair falls outta that head and it just turns up in the strangest places. I hate people to see my gorgeous Michael with hair peekin' out o' his nose or ears. So, once we were on an airplane and the sun was shinin' through, and I saw all these black hairs stickin' out the top of his nose. And I said, "Eeuuuww! I've got to get rid o' those." So I just took my fingernails and started pullin' them out 'cause they're not attached real good. I know that can smart some, but I can't stand lookin' at 'em.

So all of a sudden, Michael turned around and looked at me hard. He said, "Instead of worryin' about the hair on my face, you might wanna tend to your mustache."

I felt like I was gonna die. What I thought he meant was that I was pretty ugly because the tiny black hairs over my lip were showin'. We hate when that happens, don't we, girls?

I was mortified, embarrassed, and a little angry, too. I guess I really didn't think the criticism I'd been givin' him by pullin' out his ear and nose hairs was the same thing. But in retrospect, I see now it was exactly the same thing.

So I sat back in my seat and didn't say much for the rest of the flight. When we got to the airport, our limo came and picked us up. We got in and I was still bein' kinda quiet, but I asked the limo driver, "Would you please stop at the CVS drugstore for me? I've got to run in and just pick up a few girly things."

When we got there, Michael crawled outta the car with me.

"Where you goin'?" I asked.

He said, "Well, I was just gonna go in the drugstore."

I said, "No, you don't need to go." I really didn't want him to see me buyin' mustache remover.

But he said, "Yeah, I'm gonna go in, too." You don't tell Michael he can't do somethin'.

So I go in and I try to lose 'im and I go to the hair waxing department. I get me these sticker-on things that you put on your upper lip, and then you just pull and it snatches the mustache hair out. With a whole lot of agony, I might say.

Well, sure enough, he caught me fumblin' around through all that junk, lookin' for mustache removers, and I was so embarrassed. He was tickled that he had gotten back at me. Was he laughin'! I was crushed!

Michael: I remember that Paula barricaded herself in the hotel bathroom when we got there, and I was guessin' she was usin' mustache stuff. When she finished and came out, her upper lip looked like a baboon's butt—it had turned all red. But you know what? I didn't mention that. I figured we both had enough criticism that day. But I still remember that day and I guess Paula does too. Now I believe we try to think before we criticize the other. I'm not sayin' we never pass judgment about how the other looks or sounds, but let's each say we pick our battles. And Paula has let up on the preenin'.

Thinkin' about it, I guess another way a marriage can start going bad from the inside is when one partner never takes the blame for anything. That partner always has an excuse why he or she shouldn't get blamed. It sounds pretty much like "I didn't do it" or "You made me do it" or "How could I help doing it?" That partner would be me.

I think maybe in my first marriage, I did that a lot and that's why I say I was damaged goods when Paula got me. I rarely took the blame for anything. That's because I'm mostly always right.

Kiddin', just kiddin'.

Paula has told me she feels that there's no time in marriage to hold grudges or treat each other shabbily, to punish the other through silences, or ignorin' or tryin' to find a way to pay back a wrong you think was done you. She thinks that apologies are a simple answer for all that and somehow they cut through the bad feelings and make everything seem new again. Paula says that when you don't apologize, there's a message in the silence that says you don't care.

Frankly, I'm not so sure.

Paula is so generous she has no trouble with apologizin' when she knows she's done something that bothered me, but I admit it, I do. The ability to apologize, which I know in my head is probably a blessed talent to have, is not anything I'm real good at. I think it's partly because I learned from hard experience that even apologies can go very wrong, so I've learned just to stay silent, shut down, and be quiet even when I secretly know I'm mostly at fault. If I use fewer words, I have less of a chance of gettin' in more trouble: Not apologizing narrows down the words you have to take back, you know. You can't unsay a cruel word. But when I do that, Paula thinks I'm shuttin' her out.

I've been known to shut down for two or more days. Brandon says it makes everyone very nervous when I do it, but being quiet when I hurt seems to be the best way for me to handle things. I think I'm gettin' better, though, because Paula and I are closer soul mates than ever before. Maybe I'll break down and admit some guilt next time. And maybe I won't.

Anyway, I'm workin' on it.

Paula was angry at me a few months ago and this time, it was she who wasn't talkin'. That about killed me, because knowin' Paula, you can imagine how rare an occurrence that is. I can't recall what got to her, but before it happened, I remember we had decided we'd spend a few days away at the beach in Savannah—it was Derby time—but I couldn't stand Paula not talking to me and I told her, "You go along to the beach; I'll just hole up in my Garaj Mahal."

And that's what we did. Major mistake.

I was thinkin' then that I better drown my sorrows, of which there were plenty. I'm not much of a drinker; in fact, I'm a pretty poor drinker, but I had a bourbon, then another, then another, and by then, I was mightily buzzed.

It took Paula about an hour to decide to end the stalemate and rub out the dry rot, so she calls me up and says, "Oh, please, come on out to the beach."

I said, "You know, I'm not comin' for a couple o' reasons. One, I got a buzz on. And two, you know, if you're not gonna talk to me, shoot, you stay down there and I'll stay here, and we'll catch up tomorrow."

That doesn't work for Paula, which is why our marriage is so precious.

"I'm goin' to come gitcha," she firmly said, which was probably the only sensible thing that had been said in days by either of us.

"Maybe you better not," I answered. "I think it'd be a good idea to leave me here and let me sleep this off, but whatever you want, that's what we'll do."

So Paula came to get me and brought me to the beach. Well, instead o' me playin' smart and goin' up into the beach condo where we were stayin' and sleepin' off my three-bourbon sorrow drowner, I decided I wanted to walk down the street to where I heard some band music playin'. I admire band music. So I started walkin' down the street and evidently a policeman stopped me to see where I was goin' under the influence. One thing led to another and now I'm in the police car goin' to jail.

I was bein' arrested for bein' drunk in public. And then I think the charge became drunk and disorderly in public, because apparently I may—I said *may*—have slipped and called the policeman a pecker-head. The police frown on that. If there's one lesson to be learned from all this, if you're goin' to call a policeman a peckerhead, you'd best call him Officer Peckerhead.

Anyhow, they put me in jail for two hours. I was callin' for room service, but they wouldn't bring me anything, so I wanted out. Then I finally sobered up, they brought me my wallet, I paid my fine, and they let me out.

And Paula and I talked out our blues and we were whole again. No dry rot here.

There was another incident recently—something that could really cause dry rot in a marriage. Because I'm determined to make this marriage last forever, I'm trying to remember every day that what may come out of Paula's mouth sounding mean is just her free-fallin' way with words.

When Paula would introduce someone she admires like Cameron Crowe or Brandon Branch, or her agent, Barry Weiner, she would always say, "This is the most honest man in the world, or this is the most generous person, the most conscientious, trustworthy, hardworkin' man, the man who is most like my precious daddy, this sweet man is so kind, he reminds me of my darlin' Uncle George. . . ."

Somehow, it finally got to me. Uncle George? What am I, macaroni and cheese? I've got to be honest—my feelings were majorly hurt.

The last time it happened I said, "How come you never say he's a real good guy like Michael? I've heard you say that Uncle George was just the greatest man in the world and Gordon Elliott the kindest, but I've never heard you say anything about Michael—me, your husband, Michael—bein' the greatest guy in the world to emulate."

I don't know what got into me—maybe jealousy, maybe some worry that Paula really didn't think I was the greatest, but whatever insecurity I had, there, it was out. The dry rot, flaking off. And then Paula said the last thing I expected. "Well, you left me once before, so I can't trust you completely."

That just 'bout killed me. It was like somebody kickin' me in my stomach. Because every wakin' hour I'm doin' somethin' for Paula. What the heck was she talkin' about? I started thinkin', *I can't believe that she would think I'm not trustworthy. That she would think I would leave!* It was unbelievable.

I flashed to what she was referrin'. It was plain old crazy. She was talking about me leavin' her when we were datin'. Remember the two girls at the bar I told you about earlier? She was bringin' up the time I left her for a couple of days because I thought she didn't trust me and not trustin' each other was a deal breaker, far as I was concerned.

We'd made it all better in a couple of days. In the end, I think it made us stronger, although apparently years later, here it was, still on her mind. Paula forgets nothin'.

But I'm not so stubborn I can't change. If Paula wants me to alter plans, she doesn't even have to have a reason: I've learned that I've always got to be careful when it's apparent that she's scared or jealous about anything, even if there's nothing to be scared of. That's what I believe. Keep that dry rot out, even the *perception* of dry rot.

It works both ways, you know, but I guess I have a little more self-esteem in that department than my Paula does, no matter what it looks like to other people. I'm probably a bit more self-assured than she is.

For example, many people have asked me if it makes me even the slightest bit jealous the way Paula flirts with her male guests on her shows. Answer is no. I know how far it goes with my wife and that's till the show ends. Period. It's just Paula's personality; it's what makes her so appealing and adorable. I don't feel threatened.

That flirtin' I know is an act—show business pure and simple. When she does the *Paula's Party* thing—touchin' and sidlin' up to an interesting male guest—that's really miles away from the real Paula who does *not* flirt constantly like that, although that's what you would think by seein' that show.

You know Paula goes home with me every single night. She doesn't go out clubbin' and she doesn't go partyin' without me. I feel solid. And if I didn't, I feel I could talk about it with her pretty easy. She taught me how.

Paula: Remember, Michael, you're the one who still kinda clams up after you get . . . not just hurt, but even if you have somethin' on your mind. It's hard for you to share what's troublin' you, let alone compromise.

She's right. I don't compromise well. It's, like, if I'm gonna do it, I'm gonna do it. That may be part of the trainin' for my job; there's no negotiation. In my job I tell people what to do and they do it. Paula once told me she found that pretty sexy. Well, maybe it's sexy in one way, but if you do it a whole lot, I guess, not compromising is not real healthy for a marriage.

I learned that dry rot comes in many forms in marriage. However it appears, it does tend to destroy the marriage structure. It could be as unimportant as a phone call, I discovered.

Right before Paula and I got married, I'd talk to my daughter on the phone a lot. I knew she was havin' a hard time with the idea of my getting married, and she needed a whole lot of reassurance. Well, every time Paula and I would be eatin' dinner either at home or in a restaurant, my cell phone would ring and it would be Michelle. I sure didn't want to hurry her off, but Paula became real put out and agitated when that happened. She said she might as well be sittin' there and havin' dinner by herself. I knew it was rude but I had a daughter who needed me, dinner hour or not. Also, I was on call with my work, and they'd check in with me a lot to tell me what was going on in the port. Paula was gettin' more and more angry. That cell phone was startin' to be trouble.

Finally I got smart. While I never turned off the phone because I'd always want to be available to my kids in an emergency, I made the calls real short. I could see that they could turn into dry rot if I ignored Paula's feelings. I should have realized Paula has a thing about the phone anyway; she hates the thing. One of her pet peeves is when she's out there working or in a public place just relaxin', and someone will come up and put a phone in her face and say, "Could you talk to my Aunt Suzie? She loves you, please, Paula, and she's havin', you know—*woman* trouble?" Well, Paula *hates* to talk on the phone, especially with someone she doesn't know. So when I interrupt our private time to take a long call or even three short calls and gab and gab, it's just bound to be a dry rot maker.

I keep my calls short and sweet today when I'm hangin' out with my wife.

Here's another dry rot instigator: interrupting. Does Paula ever interrupt me when I talk? Only every time I talk. I'm gettin' used to it, actually. I know people it bothers a whole lot more than me—be careful of that one.

I tell jokes a lot. Sometimes it's even the way I tell something to Paula she may not like to hear: I figure if my true feelings are expressed behind the funny words, it'll go down easier.

Wrong, Michael. I guess I'm pretty sensitive myself when people do that to me because my feelings can be hurt very easily. Paula and

I have come to agree that we both have to learn to self-monitor our talking to each other, even our jokin' around. We have to respect each other's sensitivities.

Especially when . . . well, sometimes Paula gets kinda silly when I'm in the mood for you know what. She starts in with a lotta horseplay and making dumb comments and I get pretty aggravated. She gets tickled about something that strikes her funny at the wrong times, and I'm worse than aggravated. Now I'm gettin' real pissed off and the whole romantic mood goes down the tubes.

Respect really is the essence of a good marriage; respect for the other's little quirks and habits and needs. Sometimes a little space from the other person works wonders in strengthening respect. I may be goin' off track here against all those marriage counselors floodin' the airwaves about being glued together always, but I feel that occasionally makin' a little space in your togetherness is not a terrible thing. Of course, it has to happen when both partners are not feeling sensitive or queasy about the separation. It has to happen when one partner doesn't feel abandoned and left to stew while the other's out funnin'. But if Paula wants to go away for a weekend with her girlfriends, or if I've been invited to a fishin' tournament where I have to stay overnight, I think it's really healthy to take advantage of those times. I've said that when Paula feels strongly about stayin' together, I won't leave her for anything. And there's always certain times when I regret any space at all between us. Leavin' each other when the other's not happy about it makes room for the dry rot to seep in.

But our rare separations, when we're both feelin' real good about the other and we both are not threatened by the other's leavin'—it's fine. No matter what's goin' on we are always in contact by phone. Our long-distance jokes really keep us alive, even when we're miles away from the other, and they keep our blood pumpin'. Paula and me, we do love a good blood pumpin'.

I can't speak for any other couple, but in the end, what keeps dry rot out of our marriage is that we provide safe harbor for each other with plenty of room to breathe, a place where we're protected from the punishin' elements. Jealous friends, insistent business partners, too-tight schedules—all those are punishin' elements. There are more. Name your own.

We're partners, Paula and me. We're pullin' in the same direction, we see the same goals, we work together always. One does not try to control the other ever. Just try controlling Paula Deen. Or me, for that matter.

Our marriage is like an onion; the many layers all snuggle into each other and exist in harmony. The first layer of our onion is me and Paula, our private happiness. But our happiness depends on the health and joy of the second layer, our families; that's crucial to our feelin' that we're in safe harbor. The third layer is our careers, the work we do that makes us so fulfilled and happy. Financial stability is an important layer and it sure makes us cheerful also. There are many other layers in our onion—lovemakin', good friends, playin' around, travelin', cookin', joke tellin', eatin' good.

What if the dry rot has already started to seep in and your partner's stonewalling you with a grim silence? Somethin's definitely wrong, and you secretly think it's definitely your doin'.

Well, I'm no head doctor, but maybe you ought to talk to a professional? A box of good chocolates, a Paula Deen Gooey Butter Cake, or an armful of lilacs can't hurt. New golf putter? Diamonds have been known to break the ice. A poem?

If you're a woman, you might try a Harley-Davidson cycle for him. It'd do it for me.

SHIPBOARD RECIPE

Bridge Blueberry Delight

You'll be borne aloft with joy at this taste!

PREP TIME: ¾ hour, plus time to cool thoroughly
(about 4 hours total)
SERVES: 4 to 5

One 8-ounce package Philadelphia cream cheese, at room
temperature
1 cup confectioners' sugar
One 8-ounce container frozen whipped topping (2 cups),
thawed
One 8-inch graham cracker crust (you can buy this crust ready-
to-go at the market or make it yourself)
One 21-ounce can blueberry pie filling

In a large bowl with a hand mixer, beat the cream cheese until
light and fluffy. Add the sugar and blend well. Fold in 1 cup
whipped topping. Spread this mixture over the graham cracker
crust. Spread the blueberry pie filling on top of the cream
cheese mixture. Generously spread at least 1 cup or more
whipped topping on top of the mixture. Chill for about
3 hours, then serve. ⚓

11

A Fishin' Expedition

Three retirees, each with a hearing loss, were out fishin' one fine
March day.
One remarked to the other, "Windy, isn't it?"
"No," the second man replied, "it's Thursday."
And the third man chimed in, "So am I—let's have a beer."

I keep wishin' I knew Paula's and my fans better, and that they knew
me—the real me. Paula, they know; she tells 'em everything. What's
on her lung is on her tongue. But me? I don't talk much. So since I
have the luxury of my own book here—somethin', frankly, I never
dreamed I'd have—let me take you on a little fishin' expedition. If
you happen to want to go fishin' for a lot of stuff few people know
about me and a few things you don't already know about Paula,
that is.

Our terrific fans have sent or asked me so many questions that I
think I'll answer a few of the questions just as they came in.

Anything you ever wanted to do but haven't got around to?

Oh, yes, a few things and the list keeps growin'. I've always had this fascination with blimps. I think I could drive one, because it's a bit like a boat. Air currents are similar to water currents. You know they call blimps airships? There's only these two little things I don't know about driving blimps—taking off and landing—but those two details don't look too hard, do they?

Now that I think of it, I could definitely drive a blimp. Do I hear any volunteers who want to go with me on my first self-piloted blimp ride?

I'd also love to be on an airplane and land on an aircraft carrier. A friend is going to make this happen when I find time.

I'd love to watch a space shuttle launch; that has to be the ultimate adrenaline rush.

I never get tired of fantasizing about things I'd love to do. When you stop that, in my opinion, you're as good as dead.

If you could do anything over, what would it be?

1. Encourage my daughter, Michelle, to consider going to a maritime college.
2. Never start smoking.

Michael, what are your two greatest strengths?

My work ethic would be one. Don't ever do anything half-assed. I learned from my momma and daddy and passed it on to my kids that you work as hard as a one-armed paperhanger on a windy day has to work. You give your employer 110 percent. If you don't like a job, quit and go somewhere else.

My other great strength? Playing second fiddle to the woman I love. Someone asked me once, "Does it ever bother you being in Paula's shadow?" Well, Paula casts a pretty big shadow; there's a lot o' people there. If I'm to play second fiddle to anyone, why not Paula Deen? She's pretty cool. I'm proud to be in her company; it's an honor. Honest to God, I've never been intimidated or jealous or anything like that. All I am is lucky to have her.

What about your weaknesses?
Not listenin' when I need to listen. A lotta times with me, it's all cut and dried: my way or the highway. That's probably my biggest weakness, if you want me to tell the truth.

The other one? I've talked about it before in this book. Shuttin' down in an argument. Others may think it's the silent treatment or pouting but it's not, honest. I just don't want to send words out there I can't take back. I'm working on this problem.

Paula's greatest strength?
She is so charismatic. She never meets a stranger. When someone comes to talk to her, it's like turning on a little light inside her; she shines.

Her other strength?
Paula senses hidden goodness. She loves to go to junk shops and pick out the fabulous silver antique that needs polishin' for its beauty to show, the one that other people miss. She's like that with people too. She can come across a rough, worn guy and she sees the strength no one else does. She can be introduced to a very plain-lookin' woman, and she sees the woman's beauty of character and beauty of imagination. Don't try to put nothin' past my wife; she sees through people to who they really are.

Paula's weakness?
No is not in her vocabulary, and it's a serious problem. Her work ethic is like mine, but she *never* says no to anything. She could be

fainting from exhaustion and someone asks her to do one more thing, and she'll say, "Put me in, Coach, I'm ready to play." I worry about her health, worry that she'll be overwhelmed when she doesn't get enough rest and get very ill.

Another weakness?
No one else sees this, but she sometimes misinterprets my signals. Just because I get quiet when I'm stressed doesn't mean I want her to go away. It doesn't mean I'm angry at her. She's pretty good at it already, but she has to hear better what's unspoken.

Michael, what would be your worst job?
A job where I'd have to stay indoors in a noisy place with not a lot of ventilation like in a factory. If I can't catch a breeze, I feel like I'm caged.

What would your children be surprised to learn about you that they don't know?
You know, my kids know a lot about me; I've not hidden a whole lot from them. I think a lotta times, your kids can learn by your mistakes. And you know, I've tried to do that. I've told them, "You know, I've dabbled in drugs, but I'm hopin' and prayin' you won't because too many o' my friends are still dabblin' and doin' nothing else, and some of them have already died from the drugs. It's hard and sometimes impossible to wean yourself away, so better not start."

What do you most like giving Paula?
The guys are gonna hate me for this answer and the women are gonna love me. I so enjoy givin' jewelry to Paula. I was talkin' before about my boat bein' a work of art.

To me, really beautiful jewelry is also art, not to mention a good investment. I've already told you how much I like diamond rings, but here's another thing I love to buy her: bangle bracelets. I recently bought Paula ten of 'em. I gave her two for Valentine's Day, two for her birthday, and two for Christmas. She loves 'em and one trip of buyin' lasts for five occasions.

Earrings are also always appreciated.

You gotta keep your ears and eyes open. I told her friends to listen hard and let me know if she ever lets drop a hint of what she craves. Not too long ago, I bought her this antique chest. She'd seen it somewhere with Brandon, but she told him it was too expensive.

Privately, Brandon told me she was dyin' for that chest. I bought it for her on her birthday. To be able to get Paula somethin' that she doesn't already have is gettin' harder and harder, because, you know, we're blessed. If we want it, we buy it. But she lets tips drop occasionally; I always have my ears open for those droppin's. I love to see her excited and surprised.

What is the greatest accomplishment of your life so far?
I think I'm a man of good character. I have no patience for dishonesty of any sort or cheatin' or lyin'. I hate all that. I would never kick a man when he's down, even if I'm mad at him. I live by certain things and I'm hopin' people can tell that when they first meet me. I want people to sense that I'll never do them harm unless they harm me or one of my beloveds. It matters to me that others like and respect me.

Do you and Paula dance together?
We do some, and we used to all the time. Paula's a better dancer than I am. In ballroom dancin' she would always try to lead me, which was kinda crazy. I'm tough to lead in every way just as she is. So, mostly we do the shag dance; that's when you push your partner

around, then you roll 'em around. There doesn't have to be any leader while dancin' that dance.

Do you ever wear hats?
I do. I wear a baseball cap at work all the time to shade my face from the sun. And then I have several other hats, like these straw hats I just bought from Paragon Sports, which is my favorite store in New York. I also just bought an Irish pull-down hat with a lil' brim all around—it's a real neat hat. Hats in general are pretty neat.

What do you mostly argue with Paula about?
We don't argue much at all, but I sure don't love it when she changes my damn recipes. She just loves to change my recipes. For example, I had this pickled shrimp recipe. I would pepper some boiled shrimp and put them in a tall jar. Over that would go a layer of onions, then another layer of shrimp, another layer of onions, then a layer of shrimp, more cracked black pepper, another layer of shrimp, another layer of onions, till I filled the jar up. Then I would put a coupla jalapeños in there. So it was onions and shrimp and pepper, and I'd fill the whole thing up with vinegar and put it in the refrigerator and every now and then, turn the jar over so that the peppered vinegar would infuse the shrimp.

It was just a great treat. The kids loved it and everybody loved it. The longer it stayed in the refrigerator, the better it got.

So Paula came along and she said, "Wouldn't it be pretty if you put a layer of eggs in it, and then green peppers and carrots? "She didn't wait for an answer. "Well, I think I'm goin' to try that," she said.

So, there I had this beautiful shrimp and onion dish. And now it looks like potato salad.

I said, "You've ruined my recipe!"

She said, "Well, isn't this better?"

I said, "It's not the same recipe. You ruined it. It tastes good, but it ain't my recipe."

And then, would you believe, she actually put *her* version of *my* recipe in her book *The Deen Family Cookbook*? It's supposed to be my recipe. It *is* mine.

Ruined, dadgum it!

So, what's her biggest complaint about your food preparation?
She says I'm slow. You got to realize, Paula's worked in a restaurant, she does the Iron Chef thing for real life. She's fast. She's more like a short-order cook. I'm slow and methodical. I don't think you can rush an artist. If I'm cookin', I'm creatin' artwork. So if you want fast food, don't eat with Michael.

Is there a trip you would like to take more than any other trip?
I'd love to go around the world or even through the Caribbean on my own boat. That would be heaven. I wouldn't wanna go to Somalia, where there's pirates, but I'd go anywhere they make boat charts for. I'd like to have the feelin' for a while of not havin' an address, just havin' a post office box for a year or so.

Tahiti comes to mind. I'd love to take my boat to Tahiti. It's just a beautiful place. The water's blue as Paula's eyes. I think it'd just be paradise. Could I get Paula to go along? Probably not. Maybe she'd take a plane ride and meet me in Tahiti. Can't see her stayin' on the boat that long as it takes to get there.

Who are you really close to besides Paula?
Well, Bubba, Hollis, Bobby, and me and my brother Nick recently went up to New York for a baseball game. I love those four to death, and I was thinkin' how much fun it was, but also how there's so

many things I wanted to say but I could only say them to Paula. It's hard for me to be real close to anyone but Paula. Now, Nick and I work together, we live next to each other, we spent our childhood together, he built my house, and it was so great to spend a few days of private time with him. But tell secrets to him? No. Not to him or anyone. Just Paula.

What size shoe do you wear?
9EEE. My feet are very short 'n' wide. Paula says I have a hoof, not a foot.

When Paula's feelin' a little insecure, fat, or ugly, as women often do, how do you help her?
Bring 'er to a country fair where you can always find someone who's fatter and uglier than you.

Which of you is more fond of sweets?
Me. I could live eatin' cookies. Cookies and somethin' to wash 'em down, please.

What is your least favorite thing about yourself?
Probably that I'm overweight. After I eat 'em, I wish I could lose all those damn cookies. Lately, people are tellin' me that I have lost weight but no, it's just that I'm buyin' bigger clothes.

Do you both like to be scared? Like riding roller coasters, skydiving, stuff like that?
I like to live on the edge, to take risks. What holds me back are my knees. I hurt my knees playin' football in high school, so I don't snow ski or bungee jump. If it was up to me, I probably wouldn't anyway.

Paula will take risks—her whole business plan was a big risk—but she doesn't like being physically scared, like on roller coasters, that much. If it didn't involve knees and if I was challenged, I would try anything once.

I know this is personal, but does your brother, the priest, feel badly about you and Paula not being super religious?
You know, I don't think so. I think he's wise enough to realize that although my first marriage was Catholic and was blessed by the church, it still didn't work. I think he realizes that if we love each other, it doesn't matter what our religious beliefs are as long as we're not hurtin' anybody with them. Paula and I both believe in treatin' people like you want to be treated. If you could just do that one simple thing, you're fulfilling God's wish. That's our religion.

I see so many heterosexual marriages where the people go to church religiously but they're mean to each other and they don't treat their kids right. How often do you hear people complaining about gay marriages and *tsk-tsking* when the gay couple adopts a kid? It doesn't matter to them that the family is very happy; they've broken a covenant with God, some people say.

Well, to me, if there's love and respect in a marriage, *that's* the key ingredient, *that's* the covenant with God. What goes on in the bedroom is another story and I don't want to pass judgment on anyone else's story. I hate to remember that once I was one of those other kind of people—the kind that judges gays, blacks, other types of *different* poorly. It makes me deeply ashamed that I was ever like that. You won't find Paula and me in church every Sunday but you will find us helping to feed the hungry or to house abused women. I think Paula would say the same thing: We're both more spiritual than religious.

Will you ever retire from boats?

Oh, no, no. If I ever *have* to retire from my job for any reason, I'd like to have an even larger boat than I have now. And you know, maybe me and my wife would search the Caribbean for the best frozen margaritas and daiquiris, and possibly go on sailfish and marlin tournaments. Doesn't that sound like a sweet retirement?

Paula's gonna take some talkin' to if I'm goin' to pull that off, I reckon.

How do you feel about war?

I've got weird feelings about it. I don't wanna be in a war. I don't want Anthony and Jamie and Bobby and little Jack when he's older ever to fight in a war. But on the other hand, I would defend my country to my dying breath in a fair and just war. So we're goin' back to the same thing, treatin' people like you want to be treated: Maybe then we won't have to make decisions about how we feel about war.

What's the nicest thing you ever made with your hands?

When things were tight, way back when I first bought a house, my mother and I used to craft jewelry and toys from found objects. I had enough money to pay for my house and everything, but none left over for toys and stuff for the kids. So we'd make them stuff.

We also had a little business going. We would look for driftwood, and I would put rope around the driftwood, go get the shells from washed-up blue or stone crabs, and paste them on the driftwood. We'd put shellac on the shells and then sell them to tourists as souvenirs. You couldn't get but twenty or thirty dollars for 'em, but we had fun doin' it, and it gave us mad money.

We would also make shell jewelry. It's easy. God made them— ever look real close at a shell? You'll be amazed; you have these things of beauty. But then you drill a little hole in them, put a hook on—and whoa, you got earrings. Loved foolin' around with that stuff.

If you couldn't live in Georgia, where would you live?
Probably New Orleans. I really like the spicy seafood, there's a lotta ships there, and the music . . . oh, the music!

But I could never have lived there in my younger days; I don't think it's a real great place to raise kids. That's all I thought about when my kids were small: Will it be good for Anthony and Michelle? You got to plan with kids, then build a life with them until they can fly safely out of the nest by themselves.

What are you most proud of when it comes to the raising of your kids?
My father was a tough disciplinarian and he could and did get very physical with his kids. I'm not complainin'; I think it helped shape my character. But I wanted to do more talkin' than hittin' with my own son, who often pushed me to the limits. I am not sayin' that I didn't give him a spankin' or two, but never to the extent my dad did. Young Anthony would backtalk quite a bit, but that was part of his natural growin'. I was also strong-willed, so I knew where it came from. A lot of his friends were on a dead-end road and I tried to teach him to pick his friends a little better, to choose friends who had substance and would be there when he needed them. So it wasn't always a snap raising my son.

But listen, how proud am I that Anthony ended up in my profession? Real, real proud and happy. Today he's a mate on the *Edward J. Moran*, the biggest tugboat we have. Some natural boat people can finesse a boat; they feel in their bones what needs to be done in the drivin' and maintainin' of the boats, and that's my son. I take it as a kind of compliment; he couldn't have thought his old man was so bad if he emulated him, right? Anthony's got about fifteen tests ahead of him before he can get to be a captain and then a docking pilot. One of the tests involves drawing a chart of the depths and widths of the river as well as its buoys' exact locations and personal characteristics. You gotta do it from memory. It's a really tough test but we all had to do it.

Michelle? My beautiful girl ended up being the most conscientious and devoted hospital nurse. You don't want to be anywhere near an emergency room unless she's there. She was always a real good kid. If she ever did anything wrong, I could go to her and say, "Gosh, Michelle, I'm disappointed in your behavior, you're better than this, try not to do it again," and she would break down in tears and promise to do better. She kept those promises every time. She did everything by the book as she turned into an adult. She saved and saved to buy the homes in which she's lived. She's married to Daniel Reed, who, I am so delighted to say, has also chosen my profession to follow—imagine that! Michelle's a proud woman. Paula and I have tried to help her out a bit financially but you know, she's reluctant to take anything that even faintly smells like a handout.

Don't think she doesn't save for her children's college education—even though she doesn't have them yet. Don't think she doesn't already save for when and if those still-unborn kids should ever get sick. She is super organized and super committed to doin' the right thing. You gotta admire that kind of girl and I can't wait till she gives us grandchildren!

Got any hobbies?
Fishing, although I feel like I'm lying 'cause I never get to it these days. Lately things seem to conspire against me.

We went to Key West recently and I was real excited about the fishin' time I planned. I chartered a boat. We were five miles out to sea when the captain announced that his gauges showed we were working on batteries only and one of his instruments had already quit. We returned to the dock without ever trying our luck

In South Beach, Miami, Billy Joel invited us out on his boat. You know I didn't have to think long on that one. But before we went to bed that night he called and canceled due to high winds. So I have good intentions, but most times, I cannot wet a hook! As I write this, I'm planning a trip to Alaska for some halibut and salmon fishing. My luck has gotta turn!

Other hobbies? Gambling. I'm sorry to admit it, but I admire a bit of gambling. In my heart I know the quickest way to double your money is to fold it over and put it back in your pocket, but Paula and I just love to try our luck whenever we're near a casino. Luck's good if you don't push it. And motorcycling; I love that. I've ridden them since I was ten years old. It's more relaxing even than fishing. It opens your senses, makes you feel *alive*.

How do you and Paula best enjoy giving back to the community in appreciation for all that's been given you in life?
Only in America can people become famous and rich in their fifties, as Paula and I have done. We are so blessed.

We have many charities to which we regularly give. For example, we're very involved with maintaining Safe Shelters for battered women and children in Savannah.

Another of our favorite charities is the Helping Hungry Homes Across America tour. We recently joined Paula's sponsor, Smithfield Foods, on a ten-city tour across America to provide one million servings of meat to the nation's hungry families. Paula, Jamie, Bobby, and I pitched in personally to deliver 250,000 pounds of much-needed protein to food banks around the country. What memories we made!

We are also privileged regularly to help out Second Harvest Food

Banks. You don't have to be Paula Deen to donate to a food bank. You can help out your local food bank by donating a couple of jars of peanut butter or jelly or anything else you wish. If a kid has peanut butter and jelly to eat, he'll survive. Just Google *food banks* and put in your city and you'll find a list of food banks and their addresses. We're also working with our staff on beginning our own foundation that will be called the Deen's List, in which we'll give to charities like cystic fibrosis, Bethesda Orphanage, where we got married, and Saint Mary's Home.

It's an honor to help those in need. No one feels that more then Paula and me.

Sports? Don't you play sports like tennis and golf?
Golf is for people who don't know how to fish. And tennis? I don't know what tennis is for. I can probably play tennis on my motorcycle.

I do love to watch sports events like college football, baseball, and live boxing.

Things I Taught Paula

Not so much. You'll notice that in this book, I've said a lot about what Paula Deen has taught me. I never felt so smart in my life since Paula's got a hold of me.

But there were a couple of things I taught her.

About Not Getting Hurt So Easily

I know that there are so many uptight people you can't please everyone. There are people in this world who are just dying to complain about somethin'. They'll go see Paula at a show or book signin' and have a great time. Then maybe she'll tell an off-color joke and they'll say, "I wish I had my money back." There are people that if you give 'em free ice cream, they'll say it's the wrong flavor. I've tried to explain to my wife that everyone in the world doesn't have to love her and she doesn't have to get devastated because of a few sour apples. I think maybe she's listenin' to me now.

About Pickin' Up Dog Poop

When I walk Paula's dogs, I always walk them on leashes and pick up their poop. It's only fair. But Paula used to let Otis and Sam out by themselves and they'd poop wherever they wanted. Case in point: my house. I wouldn't have met her if it wasn't for those dogs' unrestrained pooping. She lived in a gated community and she didn't see what was wrong with lettin' 'em loose when she was payin' for the landscapin'.

Still, the world doesn't give you a medal for having the dogs that poop the most. "Paula, you have to clean up after them," I told her after we were married. "Not everyone appreciates dogs like we do."

"Well, why do I have to do that?" asked Paula. "Poop's biodegradable, ain't it?"

Sure it is, unless you step in it before it degrades.

There was a guy who lived right on the corner and he hated dogs, biodegradable poop or not. He would collect all our dog poop and put it on the sidewalk in my path, so I would step in it on the way home in the dark. Little did he know, my night vision was even better than my day vision so I didn't step in the poop. One day Paula did. She got the message.

About Music

We both always liked country music, of course—especially the song titles: "Her Teeth Were Stained but Her Heart Was Pure," "My Wife Ran Off with My Best Friend and I Sure Do Miss Him," "I'm So Miserable Without You, It's Like Havin' You Here."

Before we met, Paula liked the Platters mostly. Motown and Sam Cooke turn her on. Otis Redding and Barry White. Nice, but not all that sophisticated. I gave her Lynyrd Skynrd and Van Halen, Led Zeppelin and Johnny Cash. You could say I elevated her listenin' skills.

There must have been more stuff I taught her. Just can't think of them right now.

SHIPBOARD RECIPE

Bayou Banana Puddin'

If you want to encourage anyone to do anything,
a bowlful of banana puddin' will seal the deal!

PREP TIME: 15 to 20 minutes

SERVES: 6

One 8-ounce package Philadelphia cream cheese
One 14-ounce can sweetened condensed milk
One 5-ounce package instant vanilla pudding mix
3 cups cold milk
1 teaspoon vanilla extract
One 8-ounce container frozen whipped topping, thawed
Half a 12-ounce package vanilla wafers
4 bananas, sliced

In a large bowl, beat the cream cheese until fluffy. Beat in the condensed milk, pudding mix, cold milk, and vanilla until smooth. Fold in half of the whipped topping.

Line the bottom of a 9 × 13-inch dish with the vanilla wafers. Arrange the sliced bananas evenly over the wafers. Spread with the pudding mixture. Top with the remaining whipped topping. Chill for at least an hour and a half. ⚓

12

The Secret Life of the Deen/Groovers

(On Bein' Stuck in the Mud, Protectin' a Wife, Ownin' Stuff, Stormy Weather)

In Savannah, Georgia, it seems a man was driving down the street when he noticed a dog attacking a little boy. He jumped out of his car, pulled the dog off, and strangled it barehanded. The local newspaper editor saw it all and rushed over to the man. "Wow, what a brave thing you did," he said. "Tomorrow's headline will read LOCAL MAN SAVES BOY'S LIFE."

The man said, "I'm not from Savannah."

The editor thought and said, "How about, GEORGIA MAN DOES HEROIC DEED."

"Thanks, but actually, I'm from New York, down here on business," the man said.

The headline the next day read YANKEE BARBARIAN KILLS FAM-
ILY PET.

Paula and I have the best life in the world. Thank God we're not seriously wantin' for anything—not love or money. We came up hard,
both of us, but now we have so many friends and fans (and yes, many
of those are true Yankees) and laughs and healthy children, and
more than we'll ever need of butter and fried chicken. We both
thank the Lord every day for the bounty in our lives.

But with all the fancy, famous people we hang with, you know
what's best? It's when just me and Paula get to be by ourselves. I like
to think of this as our secret life: No one else is allowed in. As long as
we have each other, we will always feel safe.

Our secret life includes unexpected experiences we have that bind
us together irrevocably. Few people know about these, or the emotions behind them. Who knows what acts as a marriage preserver or
even just a memory we won't ever forget? We're learnin' as we go
along. We want to share.

One of the things we love to do when our house is quiet and no
producers are beggin' for stuff from Paula is to go out on our Jet
Skis. It's perfect silence out there, just us churning up the waters—a
nice, private feeling. Once we were just speedin' around on the water, the two of us on one Jet Ski, headed to Bobby's house, which is
on the back of the island. We were set on impressin' him with our
graceful skill on the Jet Ski. I was born and raised here and my
brother Hank and I explored every inch o' this marsh, but I never really went by water to that side of the island where Bobby lives. Hank
and I used to go up and down the coast, from as far as from Ossabaw
to Daufuskie and Hilton Head. We'd go shark tooth huntin' and out

on the barrier islands, Wassaw Island and Daufuskie, and explore them all . . . except the back of the islands.

So Paula and I are skimmin' along on the Jet Ski, goin' about sixty miles an hour, but she felt safe because I was the captain. Paula's nothing if not a great sport and risk taker. We're lookin' for the one creek where Bobby lives and I knew it was marked with a little PVC pipe.

I simply could not find that blasted pipe. So I yelled to Paula, "Well, maybe the little pipe got washed away." We went down this one creek. It was the wrong creek and by the time I noticed it, I'd run up on a big mudflat.

Stuck. Seriously stuck, and the tide was goin' out quickly.

"Paula, darlin'," I said, "we gotta get out of this pretty quick or we're gonna be stuck here for twelve hours."

"This sounds like another Grand Canyon caper to me," she answered.

"Well, I'm gonna get off and try to pull on the Jet Ski."

So I got off and started pullin', and I'd pull and it'd move like a quarter of an inch. Not too spectacular because I had in mind pullin' it about eight feet to get it back into the water.

"Paula, darlin'," I said, "you're gonna have to get off."

"Michael, darlin'," she answered, "you're crazy. Get off in that mud? I'm not."

"Yeah, you are," I said, dispensin' with the *darlin'* part.

"No *way*," she muttered, and laughed that Paula laugh.

Me? I wasn't laughin'. What worried me more than anything is that I'd lose my shoes, cut myself on an oyster shell, and be stuck there bleedin' to death and there would never be any way to get out of there quickly enough 'cause nobody could get to where we were. So the first thing I did was lose my shoes in the mud. I kind of hopped around and felt these sharp little shells, but then I started pullin'. No give at all.

I said, "You have to get off, Paula."

This time she knew I meant business, and without missin' a beat, that gal got off and sunk way up past her knees in the most disgusting mud you ever saw, and by now, she was laughin' to beat the band. First thing she'd naturally done was lose her shoes just like me.

She stopped laughin'.

But Paula was very game, and I pulled and pulled and pulled and she pushed and pushed and pushed and we finally got the Jet Ski back into the water.

Don't y'all feel sorry for her; she had her Paula revenge later, and that I won't specify.

Think I'll ever live that down? Here I am a tugboat pilot, who lived in those waters all my life, and I'd run the boat aground.

The next day, I said to Paula, "Well, it happened because I don't go back there in those parts much. Things change, the floor of the ocean changes. Just 'cause you're a taxi driver in New York doesn't mean you can drive a cab in Chicago."

And she answered quick with her Paula wink, "But you shoulda known that, darlin'."

"Hell," I told her, "look what I did for you. You got a beautiful mud treatment for free. Look how good you look!"

We're still laughin'.

We really have fun. We have a little catamaran, and we went just up to one of the little creeks and went swimmin'. Paula said, "Well, how am I gonna get back up on the boat, sweetie?"

I said, "Well, you can just pull yourself up."

She said, "I can't do that." So she put her feet on one pontoon and her backside on one pontoon, and I swam up under her and pushed her up. She's clumsy as hell and she isn't a lightweight, but we laughed ourselves silly.

Best of all, we like to go around and pick up our grandson Jack and go for a boat ride. He loves that better than playin' with his best toys.

Of course our life is filled with friends, some new and famous, others old and nuts. Life's so good.

Somethin' most people don't think about are security issues. We didn't used to worry too much about that, since our fans are so lovin'. It's actually pretty hard to get to Paula directly these days—you have to get through a lot of people before you get to her because we need to be more careful now than we ever used to be.

I mean, you never know. You can have five million fans write into her blog about how much they love her but then one guy happens to get sick from poorly fried chicken and right away, *Paula Deen, the Butter Queen, did it*. Most of the time, when we're hackin' around privately, it's just the two of us. But now, whenever we have to go out in public, we generally travel with a group of people, and in that group is the man who watches out for Paula's safety. His name is Hollis; don't fool with him. He'd take a bullet for Paula any day. So would I.

I almost had to prove that one day when we were toolin' around and enterin' the parkin' lot at a Publix Super Market. I had just come from a weddin' I went to by myself because Paula couldn't go.

A word here about weddings and funerals: I never say no to them if I'm in town, even if I have to go alone. I feel that those are two important events that should draw your respect and presence. I always pay tribute to the family that's left behind. I think that my mother's and father's early passings were instrumental in this feeling: I can still remember the people who showed up at their funerals; it was that important to me that attention be paid to these wonderful people. I'll also never turn down a weddin' in celebration of the couple that's about to take off on their brand-new life together. What could be more important? Fishin'? No, not even fishin'.

Paula had come to the Wilmington Island Country Club to pick me up from the weddin' I'd just attended and she said to me, "Michael, I've just got to stop at the grocery store to use their bathroom; I'm about to wet my pants." She pulled up to the curb and ran into Publix. I waited in the car for her while she found the ladies' room and picked up a few groceries on the way. She got back into the driver's seat and as she's pullin' out, all of a sudden this young man gets out of his car, steps in front of our car, and starts motioning her to pull over. We're kind of cautious about stuff like that, so she yells out the window, "Get outta the way, please, I'm goin' straight on."

At that, this guy started screaming, "You rich bitch. You think you can park wherever you want! You think you own the world!"

I didn't know what he wanted. "What's he sayin', Paula?"

Paula, always on the lookout to avoid trouble, answered, "Nothin', Michael. Nothin'! I'm not stopping to find out. I'm drivin' on straight ahead."

She has a better radar for possible crazies than I do, but now this guy started yelling the most foul obscenities at Paula.

I'd had enough.

"Pull over, Paula," I said in my captain's voice.

"No, Michael, he can only be bad news. Let's just leave," she pleaded.

"Pull over," I said. "That jackass needs to have an attitude adjustment."

I'm in a suit and my leather shoes, and this guy's a punk but he's dressed just right for fightin'. I get out of the car, go over to him, and say real low, "Did you have somethin' to say to me, buddy? Are you a policeman?"

"No," he sneers.

"Are you a fireman?" I ask, still real polite.

"No!"

"Then what's your problem?"

He said, "I don't have a problem. You have a problem, Santa Claus. I'm gonna whop your ass."

I said, "Well, you wouldn't be the first to do that, so come closer and do it."

Paula yells out, "Get in the car." She looks at the guy and shrieks, "He's gonna hit you, he's gonna hurt you! "

The guy says, "You better listen to the bitch. Get in the car or I'm gonna hurt you."

Paula, God bless her, says, "I'm talkin' to you, buddy, not my husband. Michael's goin' to hit and hurt *you*, sure as shootin', if you don't get back in your car."

Well, then he starts callin' me names and I throw off my suit jacket and start chasin' this coward, because by this time, he'd taken off. As he ran away from me, all the time he kept yellin' he was gonna whop my ass.

About that time, I noticed he had a girl with him.

"Get the pepper spray!" he stopped to yell at her, and then he ran a little further away. Even faster.

"You're as classy as your chickenshit husband, you trash-heap tramp," I mention to her.

Who comes out of Publix but a lady Paula and I both knew. It took her about a minute to see what was goin' on. She yelled, "Michael! He's drunk but he's sober enough to want you to hit him so he can sue your ass and be a rich man—he recognizes you and Paula. Get back in the car!"

Of course she spoke sense, but by that time, I wasn't feelin' like bein' prudent.

"Well, if he wants me to hit him," I answered her, "all he has to do is downshift and I will oblige him. Right now, the only way he would beat me is if I got exhausted from runnin' toward him, because look at that asshole—he hasn't stopped runnin' away yet.

"Listen, fella," I finally called out. "You can go home drunk, or you can go home drunk and bloody. It's up to you."

He ran out of the parking lot. Good-bye, good riddance.

I gotta admit I was pantin', but still a little disappointed I couldn't finish what he started.

Well. Paula looked up at me with those drop-dead blue eyes and said in her sexiest voice, "Thank you, Michael. It gives a woman a real secure feelin' to know her husband will always take care of her."

Do you believe it?

Why'd I tell you all this? Because you never do know what will impress a woman and that's how I learned Paula admired a person who stepped up to the plate when the chips were down. Go figure. It first seemed to me she really wanted me to retreat to our car so she could drive us away, but apparently not.

Women. They got these secret feelings inside. What they say is not always what they mean.

Our secret lives. And loves. And stuff.

Someone once asked me what was my most treasured possession. I've always prided myself on not being about material things, but Paula has taught me that I'm allowed to cherish, even love some *things* as long as it doesn't make me insensitive or make me forget the way I grew up lovin' God's treasures rather than man's treasures. She and I work very, very hard for our money, and we're lucky to be able to enjoy the world's material pleasures. I learned not to feel guilty about *havin'*. And so, our secret life includes gettin' some stuff that was always coveted but unattainable.

Have to keep dreamin'. Quit dreamin' and it's all over. Sometimes your dreams come true.

I don't think I'd have admitted this before I started this book, but my most treasured personal possession is not my car or my boat; it's the place I keep them. It's a garage. You heard me.

I'd always heard about the Taj Mahal—the most splendid mausoleum in the world, built in the 1600s by a Mughal emperor who ordered it constructed after the death of his beloved wife. Legend is it took twenty thousand men twenty-two years to build the Taj Mahal.

It's a magnificent white marble building built into a walled garden with an oblong reflecting pool and it's inlaid with precious stones. It is a material thing, but it was built to commemorate love. Tourists come from all over the world to gape at the Taj Mahal. I have never seen it yet, but one day I hope to.

Well, the emperor wasn't ashamed of revering *things*, and you know what, I'm not either anymore. I always dreamed of a great and roomy garage Paula can enjoy with me. More about the Garage Mahal, or rather, the Garaj Mahal, in a minute.

First I want to say a few words about money 'cause I know that's what some folks wonder about us. How do you deal with it when you're in a second marriage and one partner makes a good livin' but the other makes a fabulous livin'?

Well, in the case of money (and only when it comes to money) ours is The Paula Show, not The Michael and Paula Show. They say most people's arguments come from money and whoever *they* is, they are right. It's both great and hard for me—hard because I don't make as much money as I used to. Now I travel the world with Paula and in that way, my independence and work time is a little diminished. Great because the Queen's got a lot of money now. But you know what? We talk about everything so we can jointly decide what to buy, what each of us *really* wants and needs. We try to avoid hard feelin's.

For example, a year ago I wanted to get a muscle car, a GTO. It cost big. But I hadn't been workin' much so I didn't have the money saved to buy it. I asked Paula if I could borrow some money from her, then pay her back, and of course she said yes. We talked to the accountant, and he also thought it would be okay. Then we didn't talk about it again for a while. When I mentioned it again to Paula, she quietly said, "Well, you don't really need another car, do you?"

She didn't, but I did. Still, I didn't buy the car. I want to tell you that if I'd been making the money I used to make, I'd a' gone ahead and bought that car without talkin' to anyone. I must admit there were some small hard feelings on my part over that one.

But it's hard for me to complain about anything because, well, we have such an incredible life and most of the stuff we'd ever dreamed about.

Like our new house. We're buildin' a new house in which there will be lotsa room for kids and grandkids and friends to stay over, state-of-the-art cameras and surveillance equipment, and enough land to enjoy real privacy. It's really gorgeous but I'm already callin' it the Redneck Riviera because it's *our* house and we're nothing if not a couple of lucky rednecks. The guest towels in Paula's bathroom read, WELL-BEHAVED WOMEN DON'T MAKE HISTORY and I DON'T SKINNY DIP—I CHUNKY-DUNK.

The big house is right on the Wilmington River, which is almost a mile wide. It's surrounded with old oak trees with moss hangin' from each of them, views of the most gorgeous sunsets, and a dock house in which I'd be happy as a clam to live forever.

There's a private dock that goes down to the river, and at the end of the dock there's this perfect little dock house I love better even than the big house. It's built from the wood of a 125-year-old farm-house and there we can escape to sleep, read, make love, tell jokes. It has a pretty little plaque in front that my mother and I made years ago, and a little sign that reads ANOTHER DAY IN PARADISE.

A big wooden angel with arms outstretched and our grandson Jack's picture on it hangs over our bed and Paula says that when we sleep, she feels like there's an angel wrapping her arms around us.

We can fish for our dinner right out the door of our dock house, and after cleanin' the fish inside, there's a little trapdoor on the floor of the house. The fish heads go right back into the sea where they came from. I put in the trapdoor in tribute to the memory of my momma, who would sit in an inner tube right in the water near our dock and pick the crabs to make her deviled crabs or she'd shell beans and then throw the trash right in the water. That's Savannah recycling.

Doin' the same thing as you did, Momma.

The dock house is small and intimate and Paula says she loves it because it feels so safe and small, and she never loses sight of me in there.

But make no mistake—it's Paula who makes the money that pays for most of it. Although I make a good bit of money, frankly I couldn't afford the dirt this new house sits on anymore than I could afford that GTO. Also, I'm happy livin' right where we are. Still, we got a marriage here. We both have to be happy, so we negotiate.

I'd always dreamed of having a built-in saltwater aquarium and I wanted one for the new house. Paula asked, "Do you really need an aquarium?"

And I said, "Do you really need *five* fireplaces and all those dish-washers?"

And Paula said, "No, I don't. Getcher aquarium."

· · ·

Now back to that garage.

The Garaj Mahal on the new property started with Paula giving me that 1960 GTO Judge for Christmas last year. I call it the Garaj Mahal because it's big and beautiful like the Taj Mahal. The muscle car lives in what we call the Judge's Chambers in the Garaj Mahal. The car's Carousel Red, but it's really as orange as it can be. They only made a limited number of 'em to start with, and now I have one, thanks to my wife. If this chapter is about secret lives, that also includes secret loves. To have a garage big enough to keep all the stuff I have grown to love—like that orange sports car—has always been my number one secret desire—aside from meetin' my soul mate, of course. Damn! I *like* the feeling of not being ashamed to have the stuff we can afford.

The Garaj Mahal is a five-thousand-square-foot garage. I'm not kiddin'. My son Anthony has an apartment above it, which is where he lives, and I have a gym up there, which has very few hours on it.

Here are the other kinds of possessions I love: boats, old cars, motorcycles. The Garaj Mahal keeps my toys clean and safe. It started off as Mike's Monster Garage and Toy Box but it just evolved into the Garaj Mahal.

I can remember I parked my first motorcycle in an old barn that housed horses and chickens and ducks and geese. That motorcycle would get dusty and rusty and that about killed me. Then I bought another motorcycle, and this time, I put up a tent and I would drive my motorcycle in so it could sleep in that tent.

I've come a long way from a barn and a tent.

Does this all sound like braggin'? I sure hope not. I just feel that I want to share some of the private feelings I have about some of the extraordinary things we've come to own through hard work and God's blessings, and some of those feelings are mixed. Sometimes what we each say comes out wrong—no matter how we try. Like the time we were in a stretch limo. Paula was wearin' her chinchilla coat and she had her arm propped so her diamond ring was hangin' out the window. We stopped at a red light and a girl drove up alongside us and she said, "Hey, are you Paula Deen?"

Paula said yes with her great smile and the girl said, "Well, how you doin', Paula?"

And Paula had not been feeling well at all that day, so she answered kind of weakly, "Honcy, I'm hangin' in there."

I saw the look on the girl's face as she drove off and I realized how that must have sounded to her: Paula sittin' in a limo in a fur coat with a big diamond hangin' off her finger and tellin' the girl she's just hangin' in there. That girl was probably just hangin' in there! We were travelin' in style.

When I explained that to my wife, of course she felt terrible. So, you gotta be careful that what you say doesn't sound like braggin' and doesn't sound like you're blind to others who have less than you.

Well, Paula may have the diamond but, as you may have guessed, I also have my extravagances, one being an incredible boat in the aforementioned Garaj Mahal. It's a sliding-seat rowboat called a Whitehall. It's like a work of art to me. People hang art on the wall and they just spend hours lookin' at it. To me, a beautiful boat is art and I spend hours lookin' at this Whitehall. It does my heart good. Years ago, these boats were made only outta wood and this is a replica of those nineteenth-century skiffs. It's fiberglass on the outside, but it's got mahogany and teak on the inside. If it was all wood, it probably would look even better, but it wouldn't be as functional. It could get dry rot, and you know how I feel about dry rot.

I just had to have this boat. I justified its expense to myself by sayin' it could be my exercise boat. I could row this boat and really get slim and healthy, which I did, for the first week. Row it, I mean, not get slim and healthy. Then I put it in the Garaj Mahal. Once we get settled into the new house, I'm gonna keep it on the end of the dock and when I'm ready to row it, I can just pull it off the dock and go. I'll use it more then, but now I'm gettin' a lot of flack from my wife about my exercise program, because that boat has remarkably few hours on it.

Anthony, who calls the Garaj Mahal home, is quite an artist. We're gonna put a drawing table in his apartment so he can try to develop that talent. He can work on drawing those nautical charts from memory so he can get to be a pilot like his daddy. My son, the docking pilot. Has a sweet ring to it.

My Garaj Mahal is a dream come true.

If I ever go missin', you know where I'll be. Paula won't take but a minute to find me.

Storms at Sea

Sometimes my delicious life with Paula Deen ain't quite so delicious.

It's fair to say that when there are problems, it's usually not she and I who make the trouble: It often has to do with our blended families. We love them to death, each one of our children and *their* loved ones, but when people are melded together through someone else's marriage there is always a bit of fallout.

One thing I can tell you: When fallout does happen, it's not gonna be a Brady Bunch scenario with us, or with anyone else in the same situation.

This I know for sure.

When you go beyond sight of land in a boat, and the sea and the wind are calm, something magical happens. The water is flat calm, the sunrises and sunsets make a man gasp, the dolphins and whales play, and on a clear night you can see the stars forever. But if you're far offshore on a serene and sunny day, a rogue gale wind may come blowing up, and then you can hardly believe how fast things can change. One wind can do it, can change the scenery and scare the livin' daylights outta you.

In an instant you're in a white-knuckle situation. The sea becomes a livin' thing and tosses you around like you were a paper envelope. You didn't see it comin', you don't understand why it's happenin'; even old salts like me are not so sure what to do. Instinct must take over.

Blending two families is like a boat at sea on a tranquil sunny afternoon when suddenly you're in the center of a monsoon. Except when it's families involved, it's worse than a monsoon. It's a typhoon, a hurricane, a tempest all at once.

Family turbulence can begin on a day like any other day. Suddenly, black storm clouds appear. One minute you think you're the soul of reasonableness—the next minute someone is looking at you like you're an ax murderer. A casual statement, a thoughtless act, a funny look, a misunderstood comment, and it's all over. Sometimes the toughest part is finding out who's to blame, and sometimes both people are to blame. That's when the apologies get really tough. Who apologizes first?

One thing I know: *Some* words must be said.

Storm clouds were a-brewin' in my family not long ago.

I'm not goin' to say any more about that in the interests of family privacy, but I'm hopin' and prayin' those clouds pass by fast. Here's a whole dear family that could be in rough waters if we don't work it out.

But we'll work it out. Believe me, we'll work it out. That's what families do, but there's stuff I learned and stuff I want to say about marriage:

1. The secret life of the Deen/Groovers that I'm writin' about in this book belongs to only one Deen (her) and one Groover (me), not to the rest of the family. The kids grow up, they will leave to have their own lives, and what's left is us—Paula and me. Still, we've learned that when something happens *outside* of our two lives it may actually be anger-makin' for the two of us. And we know even a two-day rift could grow into forever. I know only one thing about family storms: You gotta keep talkin' to end any rift—small or large. Even small rifts, left to fester, can infect.

2. The family must always be saved. Time passes, wounds heal, and when there are apologies to be spoken, they really should be heard. From the time I wrote the chapter on dry rot and I confessed my problem with apologizing, to this moment, as I write these words today, I will tell y'all that I changed my mind about apologies. They must be offered.

Paula, as usual, is right about that. I know it's awful hard to do but if only for the sake of the whole family, people have to swallow hard and say some conciliatory words. They don't have to be *Forgive me, I was wrong*. I've learned it takes a big man to apologize in *any* way, and makin' an apology doesn't mean layin' blame. Who's to say who's right or wrong? Maybe each side is a little bit right as well as a little bit wrong. The important thing is to keep the family together.

3. One of the happiest times for our family is when all of us are sittin' down together, eatin' and talkin' and hangin' out. I don't want big stuff and I sure don't want even little stuff to break that family up. I know how easy it is to say hurtin' words that you don't really mean, and how hard it is to take 'em back. Look, even if you're in rough seas, you can still usually keep your balance. If it's only a little

squall, I'm prayin' that none of us will treat the squall like a monsoon and make it blow till we're all out of control.

Here's the thing: Even in the happiest of families, sometimes storms make us stumble. But the storm never lasts forever.

4. I also want to say a word about sayin' thank you, which is as important as sayin' I'm sorry.

My momma always told me that showin' gratefulness for somethin' is more important than almost anythin'. If someone gives you a gift you don't like, even if someone gives you a turd for a gift, you can flush it away, but you have to say thank you to the giver.

5. Finally, I love these three comments from the Anthony Robbins organization:

- In disagreements, fight fairly. No name-calling.

- Love deeply and passionately. You might get hurt, but it's the only way to live life completely.

- Don't believe all you hear, spend all you have, or sleep all you want.

And those are all my wise words for today. Aren't y'all glad?

Here's the true keeper of the secrets of our secret life: Paula.

She's magic. The whole world sees this funny, good-hearted, talented cook who puts even awkward people at their ease, but I see much, much more. When we met, I was damaged goods that came knockin' at her door. I was a lump of coal, and she picked me up and she polished and shined me and made me the man I am today. What's more, we both loved the polishin' part. I felt so happy with her but I had trouble believin' it was real.

There's a song that says, "I thought love was only true in fairy tales, meant for someone else but not for me." That's about the way I felt with Paula Deen. I'd been deeply hurt and I'd lost faith in marriage. When I married for the first time, I was sure it was for life.

It wasn't. At the time, marriage was meant for some but not for me. But Paula never gave up. She says she saw something good and steadfast hidden deep in me and she was determined to get at it, like she attacks a recipe for the promise of the hidden deliciousness within. We loved each other, and we married, and although the world sees much of our life on television, it doesn't see the secret part, the part that belongs to me and the Lady alone.

The world doesn't see the times we feel worried or angry and it also doesn't see our real delight and glee in the marvelous *everydayness* of our lives. It doesn't see us horsin' around, shoppin', visitin' the kids, makin' peace when there's an argument, travelin' incognito. It doesn't see us tired and spent but wrapped in each other's arms and bodies at the day's end. That part is not for the cameras.

That part is the secret life of the Deen/Groovers.

Seaworthy Short Ribs

This is great served with hot mashed potatoes or white rice. I bet it would be good over grits, too.

PREP. TIME: About 4 hours, including 3 hours roasting time. You can easily prepare this dish in advance of serving.

SERVES: 6 to 8

2 tablespoons olive oil

5 pounds boneless beef short ribs

Salt and black pepper

½ cup flour

2 cups chopped onions

5 carrots, peeled and cut into 3- to 4-inch pieces

4 celery ribs, cut into 1- to 2-inch pieces

2 tablespoons minced garlic

2 tablespoons red wine vinegar

¼ cup packed brown sugar

One 28-ounce can stewed or diced tomatoes (with juice), chopped

2 cups red wine

1 teaspoon dried thyme

1 teaspoon dried rosemary, crushed

2 bay leaves

½ teaspoon black peppercorns

4 cups low-salt beef broth

1 pound fresh button mushrooms

2 tablespoons cornstarch, optional

Preheat the oven to 300°F.

In a large roasting pan, heat the olive oil on medium-high heat. Season the ribs with salt and pepper. Place the flour in a bag. Add the short ribs a few at a time to the bag, and gently toss until the ribs are coated with flour.

When the oil is hot, add the ribs to the roasting pan in batches (I like to use a black iron dutch oven), searing on all sides until brown. Be sure to take your time on this step as it will affect the quality of the dish in the end. Remove the ribs to another plate and cover with tinfoil to keep them warm. When you're finished with the ribs, add the onions, carrots, celery, and garlic to the pan. At this time add the vinegar and brown sugar. Cook until the onions begin to soften, around 5 minutes, stirring frequently. Add the tomatoes and the wine, and stir for about 4 minutes, or until any brown bits on the bottom of the pan are loosened.

Add the thyme, rosemary, bay leaves, and peppercorns. Return the ribs to the pot. Raise the heat to high and bring to a boil. Reduce the heat and simmer for about 5 minutes. Add the beef stock and the mushrooms. Cover the roasting pan, and bake for about 3 hours, or until very tender. Skim off the grease. Y'all can thicken the gravy with a little cornstarch and water, if you want. Stir the cornstarch into ¼ cup cold water, mixing well. Add the mixture to the bubbling gravy, stirring constantly until thick. This takes only a couple of minutes. ⚓

EPILOGUE

What do y'all get if you cross an elephant and a rhino? Elephino

So here I am, y'all, typin' away in my particular small corner of
Georgia.

Here's the remarkable thing: Today, because of my newfound
ability to travel and eat and play and mix with different kinds of people I never before understood, I have an uncharted and liberatin' life
flowin' outside and within me. Because I have been drawn into
Paula's world, I feel excited and spurred on to doin' bigger and better
things in my own. New exposures and outlooks have even given me
a big-city vibe that percolates in my local Southern blood. I was so
happy just pootin' around on these calm waters, but today I'm also
free to venture outside the inlet into more challengin' waters.

Paula Deen is my heart and the link between our wonderful
smaller life and a wonderful larger life. Together we are learnin' the
fine points of love and trust and faithfulness. Together we connect
in a million different ways and share in each other's stories while
keepin' our own old tales and family values intact. We figure, in the
thirty or forty or so years we have left, if it's the Lord's will, we'll

keep explorin' the world, explorin' cookin' and boatin', and explorin' each other. We're safe harbor for each other as long as we stay close. And if one has to stray a little because of business or family, she or I will be radar to guide the other safely home.

I'm here to tell you that if you feel truly bored or fenced in, it doesn't have to be forever. Anyone can change his ways, no matter what his age. I was in my late forties when I found my door to different worlds—this adorable cook with sapphire blue eyes and a heart as big as all Savannah.

You know, I always was secretly prejudiced against super skinny cooks who try to pass off tofu curd as banana pudding. That's not right and that's not my Paula. Paula is and will always be my kind o' gal—one who knows the difference between a Northern zoo and a Southern zoo: The Northern zoo has a description of the animal on the front of the cage. The Southern zoo has a description of the animal on the front of the cage—and a recipe.

Sorry if I've offended some of y'all in this book, but I just wanted to give you a true sense of Paula and me and how we're always laughin', always findin' a way to turn a problem or even a fight into a dumb joke and a burst of laughter. Can't fight too hard when you're laughin'.

My savin' grace is that I was open to change and it happened because this woman found the latchkey to the outer world and all it offered, then tugged me through the door along with her.

Take a risk and be open to change, friend. Maybe something else will offer you a newer and more joyful life, if that's what you're needin'. Grab it if it comes your way.

Maybe if it's someone else, that someone will point the way to the kind of freedom, redemption, and fun Paula offered me. Maybe the someone else will be a Northerner. I guess that's okay, too. So what if she doesn't know how many collard greens make up a *mess*.

Whether it's some*thing* or some*one* else or your own present and beloved partner, I hope you know that there's happy, joyful livin' out there, and if you haven't yet found it, you must tug each other in new directions. That's what Paula Deen did for me.

For every reader of this book, I wish you peace, love, and adventure . . . and many jokes that tickle your funnybones. Bless y'all hearts and have a happy life.

INDEX OF RECIPES

INDEX

Printed in the United States
By Bookmasters